Bring **YOUR** Shoes

BRING YOUR SHOES

A FRESH PERSPECTIVE FOR LEADERS WITH BIG SHOES TO FILL

MARCIA MALZAHN

Library of Congress Control Number: 2019908152
ISBNs 978-0-9967971-7-7 (hardcover), 978-0-9967971-8-4 (paperback), 978-0-9967971-9-1 (Kindle), 978-1-7339282-0-5 (ePub)

Editor: Marly Cornell
Cover Design: WileyDesign
Book Design: Mayfly Design
Cover Photos: Douglas Cornell (backpackers)
and Featurepics (El Capitan, Yosemite background)

Printed in the United States of America

Maple Grove, Minnesota, USA

*To all new leaders who are about to embark
in their leadership journey.
May this book be your guide
to help you navigate your journey successfully.*

Contents

PART I: Discover And Maximize Your Talents

PART II: Discover And Maximize the Talents of Those You Lead

PART III: Maximize Your Team's Talents

Foreword

David McNally, bestselling author of
Mark of an Eagle: How Your Life Changes the World

With so much confusion about what determines an effective leader, Marcia Malzahn offers *Bring YOUR Shoes*, a book that provides clarity, insights, and actions around one of the most important roles in business and society. Management is about tasks; leadership is *always* about people. Great leadership is ultimately about competence and influence. Competence is often the rational for promoting an individual contributor into the responsibility of management. Influence, however, is the ability to gain the commitment of others to perform at their best. That is leadership.

So what creates and builds influence? It begins with self-awareness. As people cannot see inside of us, leaders must understand the impact of their behavior, their actions on others. *Bring YOUR Shoes* takes the reader on that journey. Being influential is ultimately not about what you learn "to do" to others, but what you learn "to be" for others.

People follow leaders they believe in—who demonstrate values with which they align. The leader is an experienced person who has the individual and team's best interests at heart—it is evidenced in the fundamental integrity of the leader's actions. If I witness you sincerely listening and being open to new ideas, I am inclined to be the same way. If I see you setting and sustaining high standards, I am motivated to raise the bar for my own performance. If I perceive that you care about my dreams and goals, I reciprocate by being committed to the goals we have as a team and a company.

This requires clarity of purpose—a subject for which Marcia Malzahn is passionate. Clarity of purpose is a leader's most powerful asset. Purposeful leaders have a clear sense of direction and are inspired to make a difference and contribute value to the world. These leaders delight in the accomplishments and achievements of their team and in the growth, expansion, and development of the individual.

Bring YOUR Shoes provides the tools for fulfilling that purpose. The world needs great leaders. If you can be one, we shall all be the beneficiaries.

Introduction

On a gloomy winter day in 1996, I found myself in a large, dark, rectangular office. My desk was at one end of the office, and way at the other end was the window to the Crystal Court of the IDS building downtown Minneapolis, Minnesota. I sat at my desk as the new branch manager of a bank. And the desk was empty. There was nothing in the drawers. And I had no one to help me start my new job as a first-time manager.

While I was very appreciative that my boss believed in me and gave me this tremendous opportunity to lead people for the first time in my career, the feeling of inadequacy kicked in and I felt the anxiety rising within me. I thought to myself: *Don't panic. Be humble. It's okay not to know everything. You are here to learn and to lead.* The downtown office of this bank had been without a manager for three months. The employees were directionless, scared, and confused. My job was to pick up the pieces and lead them into the future.

I had three things against me: I was young and female with no supervisory experience. I was only twenty-nine years old, and I was the only female among thirty-three male branch managers in this bank. But I had two things going for me: First, I had formed excellent relationships with other leaders in the organization that I knew would be willing to help me. Second, I wasn't afraid to ask questions. It took humility and courage to admit that I didn't know everything to do this job. So I made a list of all those people and started calling.

This job as a first-time manager was the hardest job I had encountered up to that point in my career. Compared to my boss and the president of the bank, I had "big shoes to fill." But I made a decision from the start, instead of trying to fill someone else's big shoes, I was going to be myself and fill my own shoes, or better yet bring MY shoes! I knew I had talent and the team I inherited also had talent, so together we could make a good team and move forward.

If you find yourself in a similar situation, this book may just be what you're looking for to help you succeed in your first-time supervisor or manager role. I wish someone had put this book as a gift to me in one of those empty desk drawers. But now you get everything that I have learned in my twenty-plus years as a leader and the wisdom of the leaders I interviewed in this book.

Every company's success depends *entirely*, from

inception to the highest potential of growth possible, on talent—your personal talent, the talent of the people you lead, and how you maximize their talents. Whether you are starting out in your first leadership position in an organization or you have already made it to top leadership levels of a company, knowing your personal talents is key to your success as a leader.

In this book I refer to "your company" and "your employees." I refer to you as a leader, meaning you are an employee in a leadership position, because even if you work in the top level of executive leadership, you still work for the company that pays you. I share experiences herein that I learned throughout my career as an employee of other companies and how I discovered my talents and the talents of my employees. I explain how I learned to maximize my talents as well as the talents of those I led. You can use the experiences I share here to maximize the talents of all the employees in your company—your company's talent.

I include commentary from talented leaders I respect in various industries and in various levels of leadership positions in the community. I learned from each leader I interviewed, and I know you will also benefit from their wisdom and insights.

If you start with the right people, put those people in the right places, and then continue throughout the course of the company's growth to move the employees around based on your employees' talents and the company's needs, you will have a much greater chance at success. But you need to know yourself very well and, based on your unique talents, skills, and experience, place yourself in the position where the company can maximize your talents. Ask where the company needs (and can utilize) *you* to the best of your ability. Wherever the answer lies, you have to be willing to move for the sake of your company's continued success. When you are willing to do the same with the employees you lead, they will be more fulfilled, and the company will reap the benefits of maximizing every employee's talents. I'm here to help you in the process of discovering your talents, discovering the talents of those you lead, and using that information to lead more effectively—maximizing everyone's talents.

You are a unique individual with your own gifts and talents. And in the eyes of the organization you work for, you are a bundle of talents. It is important to recognize the difference in "talent" and "your talents." I refer to both terms throughout this book. For example, if I say, "This company has great *talent*," the meaning is that those who work at the given organization are talented employees. I could also say, "You have many *talents*." Here I mean that you have many gifts you can use in the organization where you work. The definition of *talent* from *Dictionary. com* is "a *special natural ability* or aptitude, a capacity for achievement or success." A *gift* is "something bestowed or acquired without any effort by the recipient or without its being earned." It's free!

A gift can also be a special ability or capacity, a talent. Therefore the words talent and gift can be used interchangeably, which is how I use them in this book.

Anyone who has read my book, *The Fire Within: Connect Your Gifts with Your Calling*, already has an idea of where I am going with the message in this book, which can be considered a sequel. In that book, I offered encouragement and took readers on a journey to discover their gifts and identify their personal mission or purpose in life. If you already know your life's purpose, this book will help to further your purpose and maximize your talents and the talents of those you lead. I share my personal stories and the stories of others discovering and maximizing their talents, offering a practical guide to help leaders develop their skills in talent management. I hope to provide insight into how to hire and retain the right people—the right *talent*—the ones who belong with your organization from the start. If you already have a team, my desire is for you to ask the right questions to ensure you maintain and reinforce the *right* team so you can take your organization to the next level. My hope is for this book to inspire leaders to bring their uniqueness to their jobs and lead by maximizing their talents and those of the people they lead.

As I previously shared, it took humility and courage

to admit I didn't know everything and to ask lots of questions. It also took self-confidence to "bring *my* shoes." I hope this book inspires you to do the same as a new leader. I encourage you to avoid comparing yourself to others, and to *Bring YOUR Shoes.*

PART I

DISCOVER AND
MAXIMIZE
YOUR TALENTS

Know Yourself

"Friendship with one's self is all important, because without it one cannot be friends with anyone else in the world."

—Eleanor Roosevelt

The first step leaders need to take to "bring their shoes" is to know themselves well. Each person has many natural abilities that we call "talents." Some talents take a long time to be discovered, and others show up at an early age. Some talents need time to develop, and others can be used right away. Knowing your talents first gives you the opportunity to find out what other talents may be missing in your team. Jen Ford Reedy, president and CEO of the Bush Foundation, is an idea person who always had a natural creativity, optimism, and initiative that helped her to solve problems and get things done. She shared with me that she discovered many of her talents by simply trying things and receiving affirmation from others as she succeeded.

I have used many tools over the years that are available for any of us to get to know ourselves and our talents. I will describe some of the tools that helped me and why and how you can use them in your organization.

StrengthsFinder 2.0: Discover Your CliftonStrengths. In this 2007 book by Tom Rath, he explains how the Gallup Group conducted a study involving about two million people and how they developed an assessment to determine a person's top five talents that, if developed properly, can become strengths and even evolve into expertise.

The assessment lists strengths along thirty-four broad themes. The odds of all thirty-four being the same in another person, in the same order, are only one in several million. My point is, you are unique. The purpose of the assessment is to help you discover your natural abilities. Doing so helps leaders manage their employees according to their talents so they can develop those into strengths. The overarching goal is to lead your company from the perspective of strengths. Employees will then be happier, less stressed out, and more productive, which in turn affects the company's profitability. Greg Shamey, director of Charitable Planning at inFaith Community Foundation, shared with me, "Going through a tool that substantiates your strengths is helpful. I took the StrengthsFinder assessment at a church and incorporated the findings in *all* aspects of my life."

How to use this tool in your organization

1. Once you have the StrengthsFinder results for your team, you can map out the strengths of each person on the team according to the Four Domains of Leadership—a group of strengths based on the Gallup's findings. They are: Executing, Influencing, Relationship Building, and Strategic Thinking. The map will illustrate where the team's strengths are and if there are any concentrations of strengths. For example, if most of the team falls in the Relationship Building domain and very few are in the Executing domain, it's great from a customer service perspective. Your customers are probably getting very good service. But it may not be so good if no one or very few members of your team get things done because they lack some of the strengths in the Executing domain.

2. Another way to use the tool is in forming new teams. Picking members who possess a combination of strengths within the four domains will provide a greater potential for success at whatever they set out to do. The Influencers will ensure everyone buys into

the program. The Executors will carry out the tasks that get the project done. The Relationship Builders will ensure that customers are happy through the process. And the Strategic Thinkers will take the team to the next step in accomplishing the vision of the organization.

3. A third advantage of this tool is to provide your employees with opportunities to develop their strengths you discovered and turn them into expertise. This will result in strong, self-confident employees.

Myers Briggs Personality Assessment is a tool invented in the 1940s to assess personality types, but don't worry, there is no right or wrong personality type. One's personality just is. The Myers Briggs evaluates strengths and weaknesses to identify where a person fits within sixteen personality "types," based upon the degree to which a person responds in four areas. The first is *introvert* versus *extrovert*. Introverts focus their attention in their inner world and derive more of their energy from being alone. Extroverts focus their attention more in the outer world and derive their greatest energy from interacting with others. The second measure is the degree to which a person processes information in most situations by *sensing* (using the five senses) versus *intuition*. The third is the degree to which a person typically makes decisions by *thinking* versus *feeling*; and finally the way a person deals with the outside world most often by *judging* versus *perceiving*. This inventory is useful for identifying our key personality traits, which is valuable for success as an individual and for leading others well.

DISC Personality Assessment has been used since the 1930s, as a useful tool to get to know a person from a different perspective—which is also neither right or wrong. When these assessments are taken by employees in a company, the whole team benefits as employees get to know each other better. The shared results create *aha* moments as we discover how others react to our actions and behaviors. We learn to better understand others when we learn about the subtle differences in personality types.

How to use these personality assessments in your organization

1. Share your assessment with your boss so he or she can get to know you. You're giving them a tool to learn how to manage you better.

2. Share your assessment with your direct reports so they can get to know you as well. You're providing them with information on how to work with you more effectively. It also shows others how much you are like them.

3. Get to know your employees' personalities so you can mold your leadership style to help them flourish in their own ways. As an employee in a leadership position, you need to mold and adapt your style and personality to your employees' styles. Learn about their personalities so you can lead them more effectively. For example, if one of your employees likes to be recognized in public for his or her accomplishments, be sure to find opportunities to share recognitions, perhaps during monthly staff meetings. On the other hand, if another employee prefers not to be in the spotlight or receive recognition in a group setting, don't make him or her uncomfortable by doing so. Congratulate that person in private. Perhaps give a handwritten note instead.

Emotional Intelligence 2.0 by Travis Bradberry and Jean Greaves (2009) was a helpful book to me as the authors focus on discovering a person's emotional intelligence or EQ. They conducted in-depth studies revealing that people with a high emotional intelligence are typically more successful than those who may have a higher IQ but do not know how to manage their emotions. They found that people with a high EQ earn higher salaries than those with a higher IQ but lower EQ. The best news is that you can improve your EQ skills. Taking the EQ assessment and learning about my personal EQ level was a great tool for me to get to know myself and helped me identify areas I could improve on.

How to use the EQ assessments in your organization

1. A leader needs to demonstrate a higher level of EQ than their employees. Leaders need to set the example on how to manage their emotions, knowing that the first step is recognizing and acknowledging each one. It is natural to feel anger and disappointment, but it is not okay to display anger in a way that is inappropriate or hurtful toward others. How we handle our emotions is what others are watching—all the time. Yes, leaders are always being watched, not only by their employees but by their managers and peers.

2. Learning how to recognize the emotions of others is key to success as a leader as well. Knowing when to listen and when to be quiet can be the difference between retaining or losing a good employee.

   5 Voices: How to Communicate Effectively with Everyone You Lead by Jeremie Kubicek and Steve Cockram (2016) is a more recent book that helped me know myself better. These authors conducted in-depth research on how people's voices are heard by others. The main concept is that we each have a unique voice and use one of the five voices as our primary voice for communication. This book was helpful to identify the primary, strongest voice in which I communicate, and that also helped me understand the voices of others.

The five voices are Nurturer, Guardian, Connector, Creative, and Pioneer. According to the authors, in general, Nurturers have a quiet voice. They care for others and naturally help develop the people around them. Creatives are also a quiet voice and "are often drawn to new trends in ideas and technology." Guardians are a louder voice "wired to preserve and protect." Connectors are louder than Guardians, Creatives, and Nurturers. The authors describe connectors as a "genius at connecting people and their aspirations to ideas and resources." The Pioneer is the most dominant and loudest voice. "Being in front" is this person's primary characteristic.

How to use the 5 Voices tool in your organization

1. As a leader, knowing your voice and recognizing the voices of your employees is crucial to your success in leading them well—both daily as well as in all interactions.

2. It is important to understand how you communicate to others and even more important how they perceive your communication. For example, in your excitement at expressing an idea, you could be perceived as pushy and overbearing, when that's not your intention. On the other hand, if your primary voice is one of the quieter ones, your lack of participation in meetings could be mistakenly perceived as indifference, when you simply need more time to process thoughts before offering your opinion.

Dr. Bekele Shanko, VP, Global Church Movements, CRU, agrees that using several tools helped him discover his talents too. He told me, "I discovered my talents by taking self-assessment tests, keeping a daily journal and intentionally observing my actions and decisions, reading lots of books, and learning through experience." Kevin Webb, founder and president of All American Title Company, discovered his talents by trial and error. He shared, "I was very particular about whom I spent time with. I spent time with my mentors and shared my challenges with them. I also bounced ideas off them to make sure I was on the right track."

Other things to consider

Besides taking several assessments and reading books on the topic to get to know yourself, you will discover other tools as you go through life—from the experiences you had growing up as a child to how you work in teams as an adult worker. Here are some of the questions you need to ask yourself to get to know *you* better:

What type of *industry* do you work best in? Do you like manufacturing, construction, healthcare, financial services, social work, government work, startups, technical work, trade work (electrician, carpentry, plumbing, etc.)? Identifying the industry you enjoy most could be the foundation for a long-term career in that field.

What *size* company (i.e. large, global companies, midsize companies, small businesses of 50 to 100 employees, or with two or three people in a small firm or start up) do you feel most comfortable working in? You won't know what you like best until you try a few things and that only comes with time.

What type of *leadership/management* do you need in order to flourish? No one I know enjoys working for a micromanager, so make sure you are not one. Do you prefer a hands-off approach, or do you need to receive detailed instructions on how to perform certain functions? Even though some employees need close supervision, most employees work well and enjoy working independently.

As a leader, when you give clear direction and your staff likes to work independently, it's a win-win situation, *and* you avoid micromanaging. Do you enjoy a leadership style where the leader of the company comes up with all sorts of ideas that go in different directions all the time, and you go with the flow? Or do you prefer a leader with one obvious direction? Leaders and bosses who are all over the place can bring confusion to some members of the team and risk getting nothing done. Some team members are able to go with the flow but most people prefer one vision they can latch on and be part of.

What type of *team* do you like to work with best? Most of us learn about teamwork from the time we begin working with assigned groups in school. Perhaps you were the one who ended up doing most of the work, or maybe you were the one who always allowed others to take the lead and do the work. Or hopefully, you ended up in a team where everyone contributed their parts more equally. For some reason, the same group dynamic challenges are present in the workplace. We still face all of the examples above. Working with a well-balanced team is a rarity, so consider yourself very fortunate if you currently work in an efficient and collaborative team environment.

Aleesha Webb, president and vice chairwoman of the board of Village Bank, knows herself well. When I asked her how she has nurtured her leadership talents, she responded, "Coaching, listening, and giving myself forty-eight hours to find a solution to a problem. I am a fiery red [referring to another personality indicator using colors]. I am an Influencer. It's important to recognize your strengths and how to use them situationally. Coaching helps me slow down and understand my teams' strengths and create a common language to deliver messages respectfully. Learning how to work and play together is important for a team to stay together. Listen. Then listen some more. Listen to your colleagues, your kids, your podcasts. Listen to music, and read books with your children. Never stop listening and learning. I find ideas everywhere. Keep an open mind, and you will discover solutions. My strengths often lead me to believe I have found the answer in three seconds. But magic can happen in forty-eight hours. Experience has taught me that I usually find the right answer for the team, and the community, a day or two later. Don't be afraid to pause. Pausing is powerful. Pausing is responsible."

The next question is crucially important: Are you a follower or a leader? I believe leadership is a gift that not everyone possesses. However, we are all in positions of leadership—whether we like it or not at some point in our lives. I don't share the popular notion that everyone wants to be a leader. I have met many people who are not at all interested in leading—whether that would be in an entry-level supervisory position, leading a volunteer group, or leading a company. Some people are simply not interested, which is fine because we can't all be leaders of an organization at the same time. There is only one top leadership position—the CEO. There is also the leadership *team*. In a large organization, you have subsequent layers of leadership, heads of departments, and so on.

My point is that it's okay to be a follower. Just as we are all in positions of leadership at some point in our lives, most of us will also be someone else's follower at other times. It takes character to be a good follower. In fact, I firmly believe that in order to be a great leader, you first must be a great follower. We discuss this topic further in Chapter 22.

How I discovered my talents

In addition to taking the assessments listed above and reading lots of self-help books to get to know myself as a person, I discovered my talents throughout my work life. During the jobs I've held over the years, I discovered my various talents and learned how to use those talents more effectively together. For example, in my first bank job as a teller, I learned that I was very organized, that I liked working with people, and that I enjoyed working with computers. When I was a secretary, I discovered that I didn't like answering phones, but I enjoyed typing. It is gratifying to discover what your talents are as well as the things you do *not* like doing—even if you're good at them.

In this example, can I answer phones? Yes. Do I enjoy it? Absolutely not. Some people may love to answer phones and would do that rather than meet with someone in person. That's the beauty of having many different positions and many personalities and talents within a company.

When the first bank I worked at merged with a larger institution, I discovered a hugely important thing—I did not like working for a large organization. I flourish best in a smaller company where I can wear many hats and have a variety of responsibilities. Then when I left that big bank and moved to the Private Banking department of a small bank, I discovered I had to do sales. While I liked getting new business, I preferred and enjoyed building the relationships with the established customers.

When I worked for a nonprofit for five years, I held three different positions (Y2K project manager, director of IT, and then director of Finance overseeing IT, HR, and Finance). I learned a lot during those five years about all those areas—including what it takes to start a nonprofit and how to protect its tax-exempt status. By getting to know myself deeper, I discovered new natural abilities I didn't know I had. For example, I discovered I enjoyed overseeing several areas of the organization and doing these jobs revealed that I was a good project manager. Even though I didn't have all the technical skills needed to be a hardware technician, network administrator, programmer, or director of IT, I discovered I was good at managing large projects leading several groups of people. Knowing I had this talent helped me tremendously in my next position as the chief financial officer (CFO) and chief operating officer (COO) of a startup bank.

In this new position, I had to use all my talents and the experience I acquired during my entire working life to that point. In order to start a community bank, I used four key talents: leadership, organization, communication, and learner. In addition, I used the time management and project management skills I had acquired. Currently, with my consulting practice and professional speaking career, I can now maximize the gift of communication in various ways by speaking and writing.

A good friend once told me that we have "complementary gifts" and we use them together. I had never thought of this concept, but I found it's true. We have certain talents that work together well, and when we use them all at once in whatever task we're doing at the moment, we are *maximizing* our talents.

To clarify, talents are different from skills and experience. You can acquire a skill and be good at it, but it's not necessarily a talent or a gift. It's simply a skill. For example, when I was in high school, my parents sent me to typing classes. I am forever grateful for that even though, at the time, I found it to be hard work. Typing is an excellent skill that I continue to use today. You can always learn and acquire a new skill.

As part of getting to know myself through the years and trying different types of volunteering, I discovered that I prefer to give of my talents and time by serving on the nonprofit boards rather than doing the hands-on work. Therefore, during my entire working life, I have volunteered at nonprofit organizations by serving on their boards.

Questions to get to know yourself better:

- What are your interests versus your passions?
- What are you good at?
- What do you LOVE doing?
- What do you dislike doing?
- In your job, list your everyday activities and rate them from Love to Hate (i.e. Love, Like, Neutral, Dislike, Hate)

By asking yourself these questions, you'll know yourself well as a person and as an employee. As Kevin Webb told me, "Being self-aware as a leader is crucial, and using tools will help you become more self-aware." Knowing yourself well will increase your chances of leading others successfully.

Shoes have to fit just right . . . so does your job.

Know Your Value

"If you set out to be liked, you would be prepared to compromise on anything at any time, and you would achieve nothing."

—Margaret Thatcher

I spoke on the topic "Know Your Value" at a women's networking event that focused on promoting and connecting women in business. When the event planner gave me the title for the event, I was immediately inspired because it suggested two things that I fully endorse. First, the title implied that each person is *valuable* and second, each person needs to *know* their value.

As the keynote speaker, I felt the responsibility to remind the audience of how valuable they are and to tell them why. I focused on four key areas: *Know Your Value* as an **employee**, as an **employer**, as a **leader**, and as a **person**.

Before I explore each of those areas, I want to share what the words "value" and "valuable" mean. *Webster's Dictionary* defines "value" as a noun to mean "relative worth, merit, or importance; monetary or material worth." As a verb, "value" means "to calculate the monetary value of something, to consider with respect to worth, excellence, usefulness, or importance, to regard or esteem highly." But who or what determines if something is valuable? Regarding material things, the value is what people are willing to pay for the specific item, product, or service. Regarding people, every human life is valuable. Each person has talents—a special natural ability or aptitude—as described in the previous chapter, something that comes easy for a person to do. It's important for a person to discover his or her talents and recognize that all talents are valuable. For the same reason, it is equally important to recognize the talents of others. That way, people can share their natural abilities with others and learn to humbly ask for help when they need the talents they don't have. Why is it important to know your talents? Because every single talent is valuable!

Know your value as an employee

Following the concept that each person has unique abilities, it is easy to see that you, as an employee, bring your unique talents to the organization where you work. You bring your contribution to the team and your individual potential to grow with the company. It is also important to recognize that you, as a person, are a "talent" for your organization. You are an integral part of your company's overall talent pool. You represent talent, and talent has a value—which is precisely why you are paid to do a specific job where you, hopefully, can utilize your natural abilities.

Nichol Beckstrand, president and CEO of Minnesota Multi-Housing Association, shared her perspective with me as she recognized the value she brought to the organizations she worked for. She said, "I never really believed that I was the value proposition in the services I was providing. If I could back and do it all again I'd believe in myself a little more and take bigger risks."

Know your value as an employer

Many people are in management and leadership roles where they hire people. As an employer, you have a great opportunity to discover the talents in the potential employees of the company and put them to good use to fulfill the vision of the organization. Hiring people is a great privilege that should not be taken lightly. As an employer, you also bring value to your community by offering your products and services, and thus you are contributing to society.

Gene Cross, an experienced business banker and now bank consultant, told me his feelings about what he values when hiring others, "I'm pretty good at assessing talent. I trust my gut feeling. I know who I like to hire: smart, enthusiastic, energetic people."

Know your value as a leader

Leadership is a gift that should be taken seriously. If you are in a position of leadership, are you using your gift of leadership to further the vision of your company? Are you leading others by helping them discover their talents? These are good questions to ask yourself to help you recognize how valuable you are. If you develop yourself as a leader and become the best leader you can be, your value to the company will go way beyond profitability and results. Your value will be remembered after you're gone. The value you provide to your company will be part of your legacy, not only to this particular company but to the community as well.

Know your value as a person

Why do we need to be reminded that we are valuable? Because we forget. We don't hear it enough from others, not even from those who love us. Therefore I want to remind you that you *are* valuable! Knowing that you have value, and that you as an individual are valuable, is not just positive self-talk. It is a fact that you need to embrace and remind yourself about. Once you know that you are valuable, your self-confidence will increase, and you will be able to help others find their value too. You will become a stronger person who inspires others to succeed in life.

I encourage you to *know your value* as an **employee**, as an **employer**, as a **leader**, and as a **person**. You are unique. You are valuable!

The value of a shoe is based on comfort not price.

Are You a Leader in the Making?

"The supreme quality for leadership is
unquestionable integrity.
Without it, no real success is possible."

—DWIGHT EISENHOWER

A young professional once told me, "I want to be a leader like you are."

After thanking her for the compliment, I responded, "*Why* do you want to be a leader? And do you think you have the *gift* of leadership?"

My questions caught her by surprise and she realized she had never thought about these questions. Many people think being a leader is an easy task. It's not. Many focus on the outside *perceived* power benefits of leaders such as the big titles, having people reporting to them, making the big decisions for the companies they lead, and having a higher salary. However, as I mentioned in the previous chapter, leadership is a special ability, and being a leader is a serious responsibility. Being a leader is different than being a manager. Great leaders know they are responsible for their employees' actions and the company's outcome. The top leaders of an organization answer to the board of directors and the owners of the company. The leaders of individual divisions or departments within large organizations answer to the president or CEO and are responsible for their own contributions to the overall performance of the company. Everything every employee does at a company has an impact, and the leaders of those employees are responsible for the positive or negative outcomes.

Some people are excellent managers but not very good leaders because they lack the vision and fire that it takes to lead people. Other people are excellent leaders. They have the power to influence others and encourage them to follow their vision—together. Yet these leaders may be poor managers because they lack the dedication to execute the vision of the company down to the details. It is rare to find people who possess both the gift of leadership and the needed management skills.

Notice that I said the *gift* of leadership and the management *skills*. I already established that leadership is a gift, an ability that comes natural to you. Management, on the other hand, is a skill that a person can develop and become good at. Some people enjoy being a manager, and some people hate it, preferring to be in charge of themselves and not others.

Often however, leaders need to be managers, and managers need to lead. So can you do both successfully? Yes. I believe there are certain skills you can hone and talents you can develop in order to become a great leader *and* an effective manager.

Erin Procko, Minneapolis president and Twin Cities director of Bell Bank, shared her thoughts, "I used to think people either had leadership abilities or they didn't. Now that I am in a leadership role, I realize it is not that simple. Anyone can be a boss, but being a leader is different. It is a talent we nurture over time while learning from our experiences and stretching the way we think about things. I love attending leadership conferences and reading leadership books so that I can push myself to be better every day. I am also lucky that I get to work with leaders whom I admire and can learn from. I try to surround myself with people who can help me be a better leader."

Professionalism

Regardless of your position in a company, but especially if you are in leadership, you must behave professionally. Professionalism is reflected in everything you do—from your written emails, how you leave a voice mail, how you treat others (peers, vendors, shareholders, employees, customers, etc.), how you dress, how you do presentations and conduct meetings, to how you eat in public. The way you present yourself to others matters at every level in the organization and to the public. You represent your company's brand, and your most important trait as a professional is how you treat others.

Treating others with respect is critical to professionalism. You respect others when you allow them to express their opinions without interrupting and when you seriously consider their ideas as you make decisions. You respect others when you value them as individuals and don't talk behind their backs or participate in office gossip. You respect others when you do your part as a team member and complete your work on time. Your actions more than words reflect your level of professionalism in the workplace.

Assertiveness

You become assertive as you become confident in yourself, which comes with experience as you learn more in your trade and as you acquire work-life experience in general. Knowledge is powerful. Having a lifelong learning attitude will ensure you will always be learning something new and increasing your self-confidence. The more you know about your specific job, industry, and company, the more assertive you become as a person and as a manager and leader. However, don't confuse assertiveness with arrogance. Being assertive does not mean you impose your opinions on others or ensure that only your voice is heard. Being assertive means you are a confident, not arrogant.

Humility

As you acquire knowledge and grow in your career, and thus become more assertive and self-confident, you need to remain humble. You can be proud of your accomplishments yet not be a prideful person. One way to stay humble is to share your knowledge with others and offer help when you see a need. In the workplace, it is difficult to ask for help because asking for help is viewed as a weakness in some environments. But I can assure you that the best leaders know when they don't know something and are humble enough (and smart enough) to ask for the help they need. This is part of knowing yourself that increases your assertiveness level. You become an example to others that it is okay to ask for help—even when you are the leader—*especially* if you are the leader. Another way to stay humble is to always ask for others' opinions and include them in your decision-making processes. When you do this, you are sending a message to others that they are valuable team members.

One common theme among the leaders I interviewed was that they all got out of the way to allow their employees to do their jobs. Gene Cross told me, "Surround yourself with people like that, and let people do their thing."

Kevin Webb agreed, "I make sure my role is limited to my strengths. I hire for those other areas I don't do well and disengage. I don't attend meetings where I don't make a significant contribution. My role now is to teach and recreate myself."

Dr. Bekele Shanko added, "I choose to do what I like the most and empower others to work in the areas I don't function well. I am a strong leader when I am working from the space of my talents. Having team members with complementary talents is a key for my leadership practice."

Decisiveness

People who are able to make decisions assertively and professionally are the most well-respected leaders and managers. Making decisions is not an easy task, and your employees expect you to make decisions with the information you have at the time in a timely manner. That information is comprised of your team members' ideas and opinions as well. Great leaders and managers own their decisions and take responsibility for the results. It is a risk well worth taking.

Working for an indecisive leader can be disastrous for a team. If you, as the leader, find yourself in a situation where you don't know what to do, ask for help! Ask for more information, gather the team again, and brainstorm some more. Ask more questions and weigh your options. As you do these steps, your team will trust your decision-making process even more, because they will know their opinions were heard.

Mentorship

Why do we even need mentors to begin with? We need mentors to help us be successful, to give us advice, and allow us to learn from their experiences. We need mentors in the various areas of our lives—career, marriage, and raising children, for example. Needing a mentor is not a sign of weakness. To the contrary, it is a sign of maturity when we recognize that we need additional input or help beyond ourselves. The most common mentoring relationship is in the workplace, but we may also need mentoring in the other areas mentioned.

Leaders mentor others. They often have their own mentor as well—especially at the beginning of their careers. The most successful leaders have had at least one mentor in their lives. Mentoring relationships are extremely important for success in business. In this section, I focus on you as the "mentee."

Take time to find the right mentor. Be open to receiving advice from others who want to help you. My mentors helped me navigate through several transitions in my life, including leaving a ten-year job at a bank I cofounded and launching a consulting firm, Malzahn Strategic. I encourage everyone to look for a mentor, someone who is wiser than you and can help you become all you can be. Seek a mentor who wants to share her or his life experiences with you, a person who is willing to share her or his mistakes as well as the successes.

Entrepreneurship

Regardless of the industry you work in, you need some entrepreneurial spirit and to display traits such as flexibility, adaptability, creativity, passion, innovation, and vision. If you're in a growing organization, you need to be nimble and adjust to the new ways of doing things to accommodate to the ongoing growth. This means having an open mind to continue to improve all processes and never getting stuck saying, "We've always done it this way."

Connectedness

Whether you are introvert or an extrovert, you have preferred ways in which you connect with people. A lot of people don't enjoy big networking events. But learning to network is a necessary skill to develop to stay connected to your industry, learn from your peers, find new opportunities in your career, and grow as a leader. Networking doesn't have to be done necessarily in a large networking arena. You can network and connect one-on-one with others. In fact, often that is the best way to get to know another person without the noise and interruptions experienced at a large networking event. Making real connections is what matters. Making and building relationships with people who can become clients, business partners, or advocates for your business and give you referrals are what's important. Equally important is building relationships with people you can help without expecting anything in return.

People appreciate genuine friendliness. People can tell when you sincerely care about them and when you're only using them as a connection or to get ahead. In the office, you can have an open-door policy, which may not necessarily mean your door is physically open all the time (many leaders don't even have an office with a door). It means that you welcome your employees to meet with you and connect with you by sharing their ideas and opinions about a project or issue at hand.

Community

Part of getting to know yourself is to discover your passions. Who do you want to help? Find out if there are nonprofits that help that cause and become involved. You can either be involved at the board level or hands-on by participating in their activities. There are plenty of nonprofits that help people in many ways, others work with animals, and yet others work with nature. Some organizations are local, and some are global. Find the one that is the right fit for you and get involved.

Being involved in your local community is key to success in your business because it shows you care for others. Explore involving yourself with industry associations and representing your industry in the political arena if that interests you. When you apply the ideas above, you can truly influence your community to improve the lives of others as well as those in your field.

Leading and managing people is no small task. If you are a leader in the making, ask yourself the questions, "*Why* do I want to be a leader?" and "Does the leadership ability come natural to me?"

If you truly want to be a great leader, invest time and effort in developing these traits. You will then experience the wonderful feeling of leading others and helping them succeed as well. Take the opportunity and responsibility to lead seriously and go for it!

No matter where you go, your shoes will take you there.

Do You Get It? Do You Want It? Do You Have the Capacity to Do It?

"Success is not the key to happiness. Happiness is the key to success. If you love what you are doing, you will be successful."

—ALBERT SCWHWEITZER

Author Gino Wickman asks business owners these three key questions in his book, *Traction: Get a Grip on Your Business* (2012), to ensure that the right people occupy the right positions in a company. This concept intrigued me, because I am fascinated with figuring out people's talents and helping them achieve personal success in life based on using their unique abilities. The key concept in this book is the Entrepreneurial Operating System® (EOS). The EOS identifies six key components of any organization, one of which is the "People" component.

In *Traction*, Wickman created a practical tool called the "People Analyzer" that can be used to ensure you have the "right people in the right seats"—another great concept introduced earlier by Jim Collins in his book, *Good to Great: Why Some Companies Make the Leap from Good to Great* (2001). First you need to know if you have the right people, then you need to *put them* in the right seats.[1]

According to Wickman, "The right people are the ones who share your company's core values. They fit and thrive in your culture. They are people you enjoy being around and who make your organization a better place to be." His formula is: Core Values + People Analyzer = Right People.

In addition to the company's core values, Wickman introduced another set of parameters to see if your employees are right for your company. These "assets" (as he calls them) are:

Get it. Do your employees really get the concept of the specific job and role they're in? Do they understand the vision, the culture, the systems, the company's pace, and "how the job comes together"? In other words, do your employees "get it"?

---

1   You can find the People Analyzer tool for free at www.eosworldwide.com/people.

Want it. Do your employees truly want the job they're in? Do they want the new opportunity or promotion offered to them? Are they willing to work the extra hours, for example, to be successful in the position?

Capacity to do it. Do your employees have the "mental, physical, and emotional capacity to do a job well"? Are they smart enough to do the job (intellectually)? Do they have the time to work more hours (even if they want to, can they?)?

The People Analyzer consists of two areas:

1. Listing the company's core values (up to the top five) and rating each employee with a "+" if they exhibit that core value 100 percent of the time, "+/-" if they exhibit that core value some of the time, or a "-" if they don't exhibit that core value most of the time.

2. Adding the three key assets of Get it, Want it, and Capacity to do it (GWC) to the chart as the last three columns. Write the names of each employee in each row and rate them under each core value and asset.

The results are measured against a bar you establish with the minimum number of core values and assets you're willing to accept as positive (i.e. employees have to match four out of five core values and have a positive score on the three assets of GWC). Employees who match your criteria are considered as "the right people" for your company.

The tough decision comes when you, as the leader, end up with one or more team members who need to go because they no longer fit in your company for one reason or another. Wickman's experience shows that most companies experience significant growth after the wrong people are let go of the company. The other team members are grateful, and the ones who left ultimately find a better place where they fit and where they can use their talents best.

Throughout my career, I've had the opportunity to observe my employees as well as other leaders in the various organizations. I had a list of people that I called the "don't get it list." I kept noticing that some people simply didn't get it. You could explain concepts to them, provide the instructions on how to do something, and it was like talking to a wall. What I couldn't figure out is whether the "lack of getting it" was because they were absolutely not interested in the task at hand or if they didn't have the talent for that specific task. I think it was both. On the other hand, I had a list of "future leaders" based on my observations of my employees' behaviors taking leadership roles as opportunities presented themselves to them. Then I observed those employees I wanted to promote. But they simply didn't want to do more than just their job. With time, I realized that not everyone is motivated to hold leadership positions. Not everyone with the skills wants to be promoted to higher levels of responsibility.

And that is okay. These people are content with their paycheck, their job is okay (not too stressful, not too demanding, not too boring), and they're happy to punch in and punch out at the end of the day. The job is definitely not their career or the center of their lives. While I was jealous at times of their carefree attitude toward their work, other times they helped me remember that I don't want my job and career to be the center of *my* life.

The other group of employees I observed were the ones who couldn't say "no" to anything—whether they had a fear of losing their jobs, were control freaks, wanted to feel needed, or simply because they didn't know how to say "no." Though they hated new responsibilities or any additional duties, they told everyone else except their boss, the person providing them with the opportunity. These employees usually had zero capacity to take on more duties or responsibilities (not because they didn't get it, but because their plate was simply full). Yet they didn't say so.

How does this concept apply to you as a new leader in your organization?

1. You can think about employees in your organization who may display these behaviors and you can explore these tools and ask the questions: Do I have the right people in the right seats in my company? Do my employees **G**et it? Do they **W**ant it? and Do

they have the **C**apacity to do the job? (GWC). You will get very interesting results.

2. As an employee yourself, you may want to ask yourself these questions and see how you respond. Do you get and understand your job as a new leader? Do you want the responsibility you have been given in your new position? Do you have the capacity to perform the duties of the job and lead your new team? When I was promoted to my first leadership role as branch manager of a bank, I was asked to keep the majority of the responsibilities from my previous role as online banking specialist in addition to now managing the downtown branch. It was too much.

Did I get it? Yes, even though I had a huge learning curve as my first management job.

Did I want it? Yes, I truly wanted to manage people.

Did I have the capacity to do it? Not really. I should have dropped my other duties to focus on my new role and devoted my entire time to my new employees.

I learned a lot! I learned my limitations, and I also learned not to do that to any of my future employees.

Success is not based on the shoes you wear.

Discover New Talents:
What Else Can You Do Well?

"Ability is a poor man's wealth."

—JOHN WOODEN

Part of getting to know yourself includes discovering new things you like to do. You won't discover *everything* you like during your childhood or even in your youth. You will likely discover new gifts or activities you enjoy throughout your life. And that's exciting! Imagine, something new in your life that you get to learn, explore, and develop.

In this chapter, I describe how I discovered two new gifts I didn't know I had until later in my life: writing and speaking. As you read my story and the stories of the leaders I interviewed, think of new talents you may have that you recently discovered, or think of other things you can do well that are outside of your job. I want to challenge you to get to know yourself well as a person and to discover new abilities that you may not know you have. If you are just starting your career as a leader, you may discover that you have the gift of leadership in you.

Gene Cross knew since he was in second grade and first started going to the bank to deposit his weekly paper route collections, that he wanted to be a banker when he grew up. Years later, he's still a banker and loves his career.

Pastor Jared Van Voorst, senior pastor of Hosanna Church in Lakeville, Minnesota, loves to interact with people and loves to teach. He shared, "Teaching is only effective if people are learning. Otherwise, you're just a speaker. When the light bulb goes on and people understand, that's what I love."

In 2004 I felt the need, the urge, to start writing. I wanted to inspire and encourage working women to strive to be successful at work and, at the same time, to strive for some balance in their lives—even if it didn't happen every day. I thought that, because I had always been a full-time working mom and had achieved some balance in my life along with career success, I could share some principles to help other women do the same.

It was on February 13, 2004, when I was sharing

these thoughts with my husband that he said, "Why don't you just write a devotional?"

I said, "That's it. That's exactly what I'm going to do."

The next day I came home from work and wrote for several hours. When my husband came home, I said, "Honey, I wrote my first five devotions!"

He said, "What?"

I don't think he thought I was going to take his idea so seriously. That was the beginning of my writing career. I will never stop writing. I think my writing ability was dormant for many years, and something awakened in me that pushed me to start polishing this gift to help other people. I wrote my first book, *Devotions for Working Women: A Daily Inspiration to Live a Successful and Balanced Life*, in 2004 and published it in 2006.

I took the next nine years to finish writing and publish my second book, *The Fire Within: Connect Your Gifts with Your Calling*, to help readers discover their unique gifts, and to encourage them to develop and polish those gifts so they can use them to help others. As they do, they discover their mission, purpose, and calling to answer the questions, "Why am I here?" and "What can I do of significance?"

Because I like to maximize others' gifts and because I treasure friendships, I wrote my third book in collaboration with one of my sisters, who is an artist. *The Friendship Book: Because You Matter to Me* features fifty photos of her original paintings and fifty friendship poems that I wrote to honor all my friends around the world.

When I ask myself why I write, my answer is, I write to *inspire*, *educate*, and *influence* people I will probably never meet. I may never influence the world, but I'm purposed to influence those around me and within my circle of influence.

Twenty years ago I began public speaking about the topic of leadership. I always enjoyed it and felt energized after speaking at the various events. I loved connecting with the audience and sharing stories as well as doing workshops where there is a better opportunity to learn from your audience by hearing about their stories. Therefore in 2014 I decided to pursue my new talents: speaking and writing along with consulting with small financial institutions to use all my banking experience and to help them achieve greater success.

Even if you may not want to pursue a career in writing or speaking, every new leader in any organization needs to polish their writing and speaking skills. Whether you are presenting to your peers, your employees, or customers, you need to prepare and improve your communication skills.

Just as writing and speaking were abilities I had not used in the past that became my new work life, you can ask yourself, "What new talents have I discovered in the last few years? Are there new things I enjoy doing that I didn't in the past? How can I use my new talents to help other people? How can I maximize all my talents?"

You likely have more than one pair of shoes that fit you well.

Maximize Your Talents as an Employee, Employer, and Leader

"Chop your own wood, and it will warm you twice."

—HENRY FORD

O nce you discover your talents, it's time to maximize them. Start by maximizing your talents as an *employee*. Then you can move on to maximizing your talents as an *employer*—when you are in a management position. Lastly, pursue maximizing your talents as a *leader* of a division, market, or even the entire organization. We begin by discussing how to maximize your talents as an employee.

Self-disclosing, sharing about yourself, allowing others to know you is difficult for some. But I have found through my years in the workplace that allowing my bosses to get to know me has given them the opportunity to promote me to positions of higher authority and responsibility. At the same time, allowing my employees to get to know me at the personal level has opened doors to lasting friendships and mentoring opportunities. In addition, it has given me the privilege of promoting my employees to higher levels of authority and responsibilities. It's a win-win—both parties have a mutually respectful relationship based on trust.

Most bosses I've had through my career came to know me well, and they each found opportunities to promote me and open new doors for different experiences for me (both within the job and outside the company). But how do you know when to self-disclose and be vulnerable with your boss? How do you know he or she won't use that information against you or become so insecure that you could find yourself looking for a job soon? You don't. You take a risk every time you self-disclose and share about your goals, dreams, and your desire to use talents you're not using in your current position. But as Kevin Webb shared, "Established leaders enjoy sharing and helping others. Young leaders are afraid to reach out, but most leaders have a generous and giving mentality."

From the moment you are hired or from the moment

you have a new boss (not by choice), you need to start building that relationship. Don't wait for your boss to initiate the conversation. Take it upon yourself to take the initiative to form a mutually beneficial relationship. You do this by being a little vulnerable and disclosing something about yourself that would not cause harm to you or anyone if your boss were to share that information with others. Learn how your new boss likes to communicate to get things done. Learn when he or she doesn't mind interruptions and when he or she prefers to meet in person (or video call) during the workday. You need to get to know your boss in a way that he or she doesn't perceive you wrongly or think you are an "apple polisher." Do it in a way that is professional, always asking how you can help, but not over-promising on your deliverables.

Ask your boss to go out to lunch or coffee and say that you want to get to know him or her. Share that you believe knowing each other as individuals makes it easier to work together. Hopefully, your message and intentions will be well received, and you can start forming a good, professional relationship. If you or your boss work remotely, you can still ask for a "virtual meeting" to get to know each other.

As you become more familiar with your boss's management and leadership style, you can share your new ideas. At some point, you may want to approach your boss with a new career opportunity and run it by them. I encourage you to share your career goals with your boss during performance reviews when you're asked, "What do you want to be when you grow up?" or "Where do you see yourself in three to five years?" There are many performance reviews that incorporate questions like this one purposely so they can find out what their employees would like to do in the future. Your boss wants to know your career aspirations.

Organizations that have a talent management program in place strive to keep their talent and also want to help their employees grow in their careers while staying in the company. They recognize the cost of training new talent and how turnover affects the bottom line. Unfortunately, most small businesses don't have such a program. In fact, they survive by barely completing the required steps to hire their employees and comply with the human resources laws. As a consequence, these small companies experience high turnover because employees leave to pursue better opportunities elsewhere.

You are in charge of your own career. People seldom come up with new ideas to promote you out of the goodness of their hearts. Some reasons that doesn't happen often are because bosses are usually looking out for their own careers, or they are too busy running their department, or they might feel threatened if you were to want their position, and/or they think you are a potential candidate for their job that could be taken seriously by executive leadership. It all depends on the type of company you work for, the type of environment you work in, the industry, the size of the organization, and your career plan.

I created several brand-new opportunities to maximize my talents when I was in banking. In 1995 the bank I worked at wanted to offer online banking. I saw a great opportunity to work with the private banking clientele, use my technology skills, and also use my people skills. I proposed to my boss a new position called online banking specialist. The purpose of the position was to go out to the customers' homes or offices, set up the financial software in their computers, teach them to pay bills, and make all other available types of transactions. My boss had to submit the position to the ownership of the bank, and they said, "yes!" I became the first online banking salesperson for the bank.

To maximize your talents as an *employee* of an organization starts with self-disclosure. You need to keep in mind as you self-disclose and share things about yourself that it is okay to be you. You are a unique individual with unique and special talents that, when maximized, you can bring tremendous value to your organization. With that heart, you can build those relationships that can result in new opportunities where you can truly maximize your talents.

The next step is to think of ways to maximize your talents when you are the *employer*—the supervisor or manager. As I shared already, allowing my employees to get to know me as a person helped them understand me more. I shared about my personality, why I do the things the way I do, how I like to communicate with them, when I'm most productive during the day, and when I'm most available for minor issues. Of course, my employees always knew they could interrupt me during the day for any related customer or bank-related crisis. But these circumstances were very rare.

One of the things I did with my direct reports was to give them a one-hour weekly meeting where I devoted my time only to them and their departments. If we didn't have anything to discuss, we used the time to get to know each other. I even learned the names of their pets! Forming these relationships with my employees helped me lead them more successfully. They knew I had their best interests at heart.

When you are the boss, there are certain talents you need to use. Right now I'm referring to talents such as communication, organization, and leadership, for example. Every supervisor and manager is in a leadership position, so if leadership doesn't come natural to you, you will need to work harder at learning and developing leadership skills. Notice I didn't say at developing the leadership *gift*. The point here is that you can be in a position of leadership without having the gift of leadership. It will be harder for you, but you can do it.

Other skills that you need to develop and learn to be a successful manager include management skills, negotiation skills, and presentation skills, for example. As a manager, you need to learn the human resources/employment laws so your company isn't sued by employees due to your lack of knowledge in the legal area in regard to employment. In addition, you need to know the skills and be proficient at everything it takes to do your specific job in your field. A good example here could be a nurse supervisor. He or she must have the education. In this case, a nursing degree. He or she must also have developed the nursing skills to conduct certain procedures, know how to administer drugs to patients, and know how to chart the patients effectively and accurately. I call these "job-related skills" and not management skills. Most of these skills are developed directly through work experience.

When you are in a position of leadership, you have an opportunity to delegate and outsource the talents you do not possess. That's why it's good to know yourself and the talents you do have. Once you know that, you can surround yourself with people who have the talents you're missing, and you'll form an amazing team. It is okay to admit you don't have certain skills. For example, when I was a bank CFO, I hired a financial assistant to whom I delegated all the tasks I could delegate—including my favorite tasks, such as doing the budgets of the bank. Years later we hired a new financial assistant and I promoted the first employee to controller. There were many spread-sheets I could have developed, but it would have taken me more time than it took our new financial assistant. I knew both of these employees had more proficient Excel skills, so I delegated those tasks to them. We didn't have marketing expertise at the bank, so we outsourced that skill to a professional with the time and talent to perform those tasks. As a writer, could I have spent my time writing a marketing brochure? Maybe, but it would have taken me a long time since I don't have that talent or experience, nor the education in marketing.

Director Greg Shamey said it well when I asked him how he maximized his talents. He responded, "I'm an analytical person. In my current job, I take the data and analyze it first, then I tell the story to the team and/or the board of directors." Greg does not consider himself a technical person but, since he was in school and later in college, he discovered he's good at identifying people's assignments and keeping them accountable. Now, as a manager, he maximizes that ability to keep others accountable.

Lastly, to maximize your talents as a *leader* means to maximize your top goal—to influence others. How do you influence your employees, your peers, the executive leadership of your organization, your board of directors if you have access to them, and everyone else you need to work with as the leader? How do you influence your customers (when you're selling), your vendors (when you're negotiating contracts), or your community (when it comes to your company's reputation)? You do it in a variety of ways such as your words, your actions, and by maximizing *all* your talents.

Nichol Beckstrand influences others by incorporating three key leadership skills she learned from three different individuals who influenced her as a leader. She said, "I have made it a point to spend time with individuals I have gained leadership skills from. As I look at my career, there are three individuals that have guided me in my leadership. One taught me the value of working hard, the second nurtured me in the art of negotiation, and the third showed me how to foster valued relationships. I have taken every opportunity I could to spend time with these individuals and study their mastery of these skills. I recognize the need to incorporate these three skills into my leadership style because continued refinement of them is necessary."

If you are a leader and you know you also have the *gift* of leadership, you are privileged. You have a great gift that not every person in a leadership position possesses. Sadly, in many cases, everyone recognizes if the person in the leadership position is *not* a leader except that person. If you have the gift of leadership, treat this gift with the utmost respect and accept the responsibility that comes with it. Imagine—you have the power and privilege to influence what others think and do based on how you lead them and based on your message.

How do you maximize this gift of leadership? By being a person of character and integrity—knowing yourself well and staying true to yourself. You maximize your influence when you inspire others and encourage others to never give up in well doing. You lead from a perspective of loving and caring for those you lead. You lead from the heart, knowing you made the best decisions with the information you had at the time and by having the best interests of the people you represent at heart.

You may be thinking, *That's easier said than done*. It is easy actually—when you stay true to yourself and not violate your own core values or the core values of your organization. In some cases, you will need to be prepared to lose your job. But that's okay. You can leave in peace, knowing your conscience is clean. The truth always comes out, and you can walk away knowing in your heart that you did the best you could. You did the right thing. You will get another job, and you will be fine. You will also leave a legacy of being a person of character and integrity—an example to other leaders who will follow in your footsteps and they will be told, "You have big shoes to fill." You will become a leader of leaders. That's how you maximize *your* talents as a *leader*.

Choose and buy your OWN shoes.

New Job? "Big Shoes to Fill"? Bring YOUR Shoes!

"When you are authentic, genuine, know yourself, and act as yourself wherever you go, people will like you more. You won't be under any stress to be someone else."

—MARCIA MALZAHN

So you did such a good job at self-disclosing that you got a promotion or you simply found a new job somewhere else where your talents can be maximized. In your new position, you have a great opportunity to continue to develop those talents.

When first starting a new job, most people fear being compared to the person who occupied that position previously, especially if it's a leadership position. It is common to compare the previous person to the new one and to compare ourselves if we are the new person. We not only compare ourselves in personality and leadership styles, but also in what kind of legacy we will leave when it is our turn to move on.

In my previous roles as HR director for both a non-profit and a for-profit organization, and as board chair of a nonprofit, I had the opportunity to hire people for various positions at all levels. I conducted interviews on my own but usually went through the process with a team of people. During those types of interviews, almost every candidate hears the words, "You have big shoes to fill." After a while I thought those words could be discouraging to the interviewees. So I started encouraging the candidates to instead "Bring *your* shoes!" We are each unique, with our own set of skills, experiences, and talents that we bring to a job. Every person is a unique and different package.

Keep this wisdom in mind if you are in transition right now and looking to "fill someone else's shoes."

Be authentic. Bring yourself to the interview and, if you get the job, bring yourself to the job. Even the strangers you meet at the interview can notice and sense if you are not authentic. Being authentic means being reliable, true, dependable, and trustworthy. These character traits show up when employers follow up on references prior to hiring. Being authentic usually means you behave the same at work and at home. You are yourself wherever you go and whoever you're with.

Be genuine. Being genuine means being honest, sincere, open, and candid. During an interview you have plenty of opportunities to exaggerate your previous experiences, be dishonest or insincere about a previous experience, and even be tempted to lie. Don't. People can figure it out. Your body language changes when not telling the truth. Be genuine and truthful.

Be yourself. As mentioned above, bring the real you to the meeting. It's okay to be yourself. The more you know yourself, the easier it will be for you to embrace who you are and accept yourself. Discover your weaknesses and strengths, and maximize your strengths. Develop your talents so they become strengths. Make sure you look for a job that suits your personality, ability, experience, and talents. That's where you will have the best chances for success. Be okay being YOU!

Be proud of who you are. When you are authentic, genuine, know yourself, and act as yourself wherever you go, people will like you more. You won't be under any stress to be someone else. List all the things you have accomplished in your life. Remember your previous successes and celebrate. Remember your failures as well and what you learned from them. Be proud that you survived your failures and were able to move on to today. You can be proud of who you are and where you came from yet be a humble person. It means you recognize that you are a human being who made mistakes and has also experienced accomplishments throughout your life.

Avoid comparing yourself to others. The number-one way you can make yourself feel bad about yourself is to compare yourself to others. Why? Because you will *never* be anyone else other than *you*! And that is okay. If you are in a leadership position, it is crucially important that you not compare yourself to other leaders in your organization. You should only compare yourself to you and see how you have improved each year, each month, and each day. You can look up to other leaders and your mentors, but that is different than *comparing* yourself to them. You can learn from them and even imitate certain behaviors you admire, but you need to always be yourself. Lastly, when you don't compare yourself to others, and embrace the person you are—physically, emotionally, and professionally—you become more confident in who you are.

Looking at this topic from the other side of the table, as a manager, you may be the person interviewing others. Avoid comparing candidates to the previous person who occupied that position regardless of which position you're hiring for. Focus instead on the attributes you want the new employee to have in order to take the organization to the next level and continue to fulfill the vision and mission of the company. Comparing the new employee with the previous one can only set that person up for failure and decrease his or her self-esteem.

As Erin Procko said when I asked her what advice she would give her younger self, "Don't be afraid of new challenges. Every time I have taken a risk was when I grew the most. Be confident and don't undervalue your abilities; authenticity is powerful. Don't be intimidated just because everyone else in the room may be older than you, but take the time to learn from those with more experience. Be a sponge, everything you learn will come in handy in some situation in the future, you just don't know when. Every person you meet matters, make sure you build your network and stay in touch with your network. Lastly, don't ever compromise your values or beliefs."

If you are the one *chosen* to fill someone else's shoes, don't be afraid. You can do it! That company, committee, HR rep, or manager chose you because they saw something in you. They saw potential and wanted to have you as part of their team. Remember, bring *your* shoes and maximize *your* talents!

There is nothing like authentic, genuine, custom-made shoes.

Does Your Workplace Allow You to Flourish as an Employee?

"As we let our own light shine, we unconsciously give other people permission to do the same."

—NELSON MANDELA

To maximize your talents, you need to work in an environment that allows you to do that. Do you work in a place where your gifts and talents are valued and appreciated and also allowed to flourish? Even though this is the ideal work scenario, you may not end up in a company that has that kind of culture. However, as an employee, you can create an environment where you can flourish even when your manager or the organization does not provide it for you. Here are some strategies you can use.

Create new opportunities. You can create opportunities for yourself by proposing new ideas. For example, early in my career, when I worked in the cash management department of a bank, I saw a need to have a position dedicated to servicing business clients. I wrote a job description for a cash management representative position and presented it to my boss. I told him I was the only candidate for the job and that I was ready to move into it. He approved it, and I got promoted. I have to say though that in this department and with my boss at the time, I had the perfect environment to flourish and use many of my talents. My boss was the kind of person who allowed his employees to succeed, and he provided opportunities to all the employees in his department.

Sometimes you need several factors to work together such as timing and your own readiness. You have to prepare yourself for a while so you are ready for the new job when it opens up. You must time it right with the needs of the organization. Learning to do both takes time as you acquire strategic skills to manage your career.

Initiate the conversation. Let your manager know you are interested in doing additional duties even if they are beyond the scope of your job. This tells your manager that you are willing to learn and not afraid to try new things. Jen Ford Reedy is a great example of initiating the conversation and thus change. As a leader of a large non-profit foundation, Jen understands her influence on people and has made significant contributions to the Itasca Project in Minneapolis, Minnesota. She shared, "What I do best, is collaborative problem-solving—getting people together to figure out how to solve problems for the community." She initiated conversations that created opportunities for her and others to flourish.

On several occasions I offered to perform duties without getting paid that were beyond my job description and above my pay scale. For example, I volunteered to attend conferences that were meant for the board directors, not for the CFO. I offered to go and come back with a summary of the most important information to train the directors. It was a win-win. They didn't have to go, and I learned and got to train them. I initiated those conversations, and new doors opened for me.

Self-disclose. As stressed previously, it's important to first get to know yourself by taking several assessments on your own and sharing them with your managers so they learn more about you. Most managers will appreciate it and gain from knowing you better. At some point in our working lives, most of us will encounter a bad manager who has no interest in developing his/her employees, but such managers are hopefully the exceptions. Part of self-disclosure is sharing the type of organizational culture you work best in. Self-disclosure can open new doors for you and create an environment where you can flourish.

Ask Questions. Ask questions about your position to clarify your job expectations and role. Ask your manager how she or he wants you to do certain tasks, and what's their preferred communication style (i.e. Do they prefer to discuss a matter in person, by email, or phone? What time do they prefer to meet during the day?). As Melissa Johnston, senior vice president of Commercial Banking at Highland Bank shared when I asked her for one piece of advice she would give her younger self, "When someone asks you to do something, it's important to find out when they want the assignment done by. As a young professional, I often put unreasonable expectations on myself to get things done for people as fast as I could, when the reality was they didn't need it for another few days or even a week. Whether it's a client, coworker, or manager, I learned to ask, 'By when were you looking to have a response on this?' and 90 percent of the time, I found out that I had more time than I expected. This has allowed me to manage my own schedule better and reduce internal stress."

As an employee, enjoy your job, learn everything you can from it while you're there, and explore new opportunities right where you are. In Part II, we discuss how you can allow your *employees* to flourish when you are in a leadership position.

If you bring your shoes, others will too.

Inspiration:
A Rare Treasure

"Disneyland will never be completed. It will continue to grow as long as there is imagination left in the world."

—WALT DISNEY

Adding to the previous chapter (where employees need to have an environment where they can flourish), is another key ingredient to that environment: Inspiration.

Have you ever felt inspired? How often do you feel the inspiration within you? Somedays I feel inspired to write, and write, and write. I have so many ideas in my head coming from my heart that I feel I'm going to burst if I don't get them out. The word "inspire" means "to fill with an animating, quickening, or exalting influence; to produce or arouse (a feeling, thought, etc.); to fill or affect with a specified feeling, thought, etc.; to influence or impel; to animate, as an influence, feeling, thought, or the like, does; to communicate or suggest by a divine or supernatural influence; to guide or control by divine influence" (Dictionary.com). Note some key words here: "to fill," "animating," "feeling," and "influence." I pick those words because, when I feel *inspired*, I am often *influenced* by something I did or read, or by someone I heard speak that triggered *feelings* and thoughts that *animated* and *filled* me. Words were sown into my heart that produced a fire within me that I could not contain.

In this chapter, I simply want to inspire and motivate you to become further inspired! Certain circumstances and some activities produce strong moments that trigger inspiration in my life. I think a lot before I start a new project, act on a new idea, or respond to a complex problem to solve. During that brainstorming time, I create scenarios in my mind that could be possible solutions to the problem at hand. Or I brainstorm about brand new ideas. For example, ideas for a new book include questions such as: Why do I want to write *this* book? Who will it help? Who would my audience be? Can I speak about that subject to encourage people to read the book? If I have answers to all those questions, I write down the idea/concept for the new book and put it aside until I start writing.

My early training on computer programming probably helped me to think a lot first, then organize my thoughts in a logical way, and ask a lot of questions before starting something. That process caused me to create an organized, well-thought-out product (or project) in the end. But most of all, I find I need time to *think*; and from thinking comes the *inspiration*. Therefore I need to ensure that I have the time to think and the right environment to do it in.

Our lives are more often filled with busyness—both at work and at home—rather than inspiration. No time to think. Inspiration is a rare treasure that can rekindle our lives in remarkable ways when we find it. And inspiration in the workplace? That's something you don't hear about often. Although there are a few companies that recognize the need for employees to have time to explore, brainstorm, share ideas, and test various scenarios without suffering the consequences of "lost productive time" or being looked down at as wasting time "goofing off."

Regardless of where you work, if you want to become inspired in your life, here are a few things that work for me that may help you too.

- Make the time to simply think. Examples of how you can make time could be going for a walk, thinking while you drive instead of being on the phone, or allocating time once a week to be still and think.

- Find those circumstances—a place, certain music, specific scenery—that take you to a place of inspiration. Once you find them, repeat them intentionally.

- Write down your thoughts immediately when you feel inspired. You will likely lose ideas if you wait until later. Keep a pad of paper and pen in your car, next to your bed, in the bathroom, etc., that is accessible on a moment's notice. Keep a recorder in the car or record your thoughts in your smartphone as they come.

- Volunteer to do a project you've never done at work. Your inspiration will get going when thinking about how to do something new. The project could be something as simple as volunteering to create the PowerPoint file for a group presentation. If you don't know how to use this software, it will be a great opportunity to learn. Be careful not to over-commit and be strategic about the type of projects you choose to take on.

- Take a class at the community center on something you've always wanted to do (i.e. dancing, swimming, computers, writing, pottery, carpentry, social media, self-defense, etc.).

- Take on a new hobby or sport such as golf, running, skiing, snowmobiling, photography, biking, sewing, quilting, etc.

- Redecorate your house or a room in your house. Doing so will make you think of new ways to arrange the furniture, paint the walls a new color, and find inexpensive ways to be creative.

- Exercise regularly. Exercising clears your mind, reduces stress hormones, promotes better sleep, and all of those things in turn help you become inspired easier.

- Attend conferences in your industry so you can listen to inspiring motivational speakers. Their job is to *inspire* you! As an inspirational speaker myself, that is my number-one priority when I'm hired to speak at conferences. Attending conferences makes you feel part of something bigger than yourself and helps you to not feel alone.

- Lastly, get to know other professionals in your community and in your industry. There are plenty of professionals, business leaders, and entrepreneurs who want to make a difference. Listening to their stories will inspire you to also work with passion and make a significant impact in your community. Doing so will be part of your legacy as a business professional in your country and in the world.

Inspiration begets creativity. Everyone is creative in one way or another. I used to think I wasn't creative simply because I don't consider myself an artsy person or have any imagination for decorating my house or knowing how colors work together. I know what I like once I see it put together, but I let people with those gifts help me in those areas. I worked my whole career in jobs where I used other talents such as working with numbers and utilizing organization, communication, and leadership talents. When I worked on the bank startup, I had to use incredible creativity in order to build the various departments from scratch. Those opportunities were great, but I was missing a refreshing side, something that would clear my head from the overwhelming amount of work I had. I found the solution when I started writing. I discovered I do have a creative side in me. I started writing every weekend and found that on Mondays I felt refreshed, renewed, and excited to be at work to start the week.

I also joined the board of a local nonprofit, Minnesota Center for Book Arts (MCBA), and just being around creative people inspired me to write *The Friendship Book*. That book was as a result of working with the people of MCBA and learning about book art, which is simply to display art in book form. I started writing friendship poems and planned to publish the book with just the poems. But then I had an idea: why not include art in this book? That's how I decided to include my sister's art and collaborate with her.

Any new leader will need to use creativity in many areas. One area is to maximize the talents of your overall entire team by placing each person on the appropriate team based on the projects you must complete. Another way you can be creative is by allowing flexible schedules to those who need it, getting the workload done while not upsetting the other team members who don't need the flexibility.

In what ways are you creative? I encourage you to discover your own creativity and find ways to develop those talents. I hope you find your inspirational sources so you can possess this rare treasure—inspiration—and live a more fulfilling life as you develop your creative side.

Imagine where your shoes can take you if you only let them walk you there . . .

Volunteering: Waste of Time or Amazing Opportunity?

"We make a living by what we get. We make a life by what we give."

—Winston Churchill

You won't always have the opportunity to use all your talents in the company you work for. If you are fortunate, you will be able to use at least one or two of your talents. But regardless of how many talents you get to use at your job, you will be more fulfilled if you can expand and develop your other talents outside of work. The best way you can do this is by volunteering in a nonprofit organization whose vision and beliefs align with yours. Nonprofits are always looking for volunteers, and you will learn from them and experience the amazing satisfaction of helping others.

When I asked Heidi Gesell, president and CEO of Bank Cherokee, how she nurtured her talents, she said, "by listening to and observing leaders with a variety of styles, reading about leadership, attending seminars as a way to gather ideas; and then taking some of those ideas and adapting them to our organization, and volunteering for leadership positions in other organizations."

I asked her for one piece of advice she would give her younger self, and she suggested, "Take on challenges. Offer to help with projects, especially in other areas of the organization. Take advantage of opportunities to learn. Connect with people throughout the organization. Volunteer."

Do you want to join our board of directors? That's a question you don't hear every day, but it may happen when people see you have a heart to help others and the talent to do so. Nonprofit organizations are always seeking potential board members to bring their business experience, talents, and hearts into their organizations. In 1993, I first joined a nonprofit board as a volunteer. My first position was Education & Training chair for Financial Women International (FWI), a nonprofit association with the mission to empower women in the financial services industry. A few months later, the treasurer resigned due to family health issues, and I was asked to step into that role even though I had only just joined the board. I gladly accepted because I love working with numbers, and I saw it as a great opportunity to get to know the organization better. I served on the FWI board on various positions over the next sixteen years. I was elected president of the local chapter twice and served as a director of the national board.

During my time volunteering with FWI, I made lifelong friends and business connections that are still active today. I received formal training on the Roberts Rules of Order, how to conduct effective board meetings, and how to lead a nonprofit association made up only of volunteers. I learned to work in teams, hired speakers for our programs, and wrote monthly newsletter articles. In short, I learned many of the "soft skills" leaders need to be successful.

While I was the president of the FWI's Downtown Exchange Group leading 133 members, I completed the Management Certification Program they offered. At the end of my term, my manager at the bank where I was working at the time came to my office and said, "Marci, let's talk management." She said that because of my willingness to volunteer to lead the association, and because I had obtained the Management Certification through FWI's Program, she felt I was ready to lead the bank's branch in downtown Minneapolis. I was surprised to be asked since I had never supervised anyone up to that point (and I still didn't have my college degree), but I was very grateful for the new opportunity.

During my time at that bank, I volunteered to participate in the annual Juvenile Diabetes Foundation fundraising effort. My strategy was to ask all the senior executives and owners to support me so I could raise the most amount of money and win the contest. And I won. The reward was dinner with the owners of the bank. Because of my willingness to volunteer, I was now being recognized and became more visible in the organization.

Since I started volunteering on boards, I have made my individual contribution of "the four T's" of connection: time, talent, treasure, and touch. At the same time, each nonprofit organization I've worked with made a contribution back into my life. We always think we're the ones helping them, but we receive so much more in return.

There are many types of volunteer opportunities. You can volunteer to work directly with an organization's clients or work behind the scenes to help with administration or in the warehouse organizing donated items. There are countless ways you can be involved just as there are countless nonprofit organizations that can use your help and talents. The best way to decide where to help is by asking yourself the question: *Who* do I want to help? Then look for an organization that helps those people and get involved if their beliefs align with yours. The "who" also includes volunteering to help animals such as with the local humane society or animal rescue organization. Here are some examples of organizations, grouped by theme, that you could get involved in that I've had great experience working with.

Art:

- **Minnesota Center for Book Arts:** Volunteer at one of their events. www.mnbookarts.org

Children and youth:

- **Big Brothers Big Sisters:** Become a "Big" and mentor a child. Participate in their programs so Bigs and Littles can have fun together. www.bigstwincities.org

- **Feed My Starving Children:** Go with friends or coworkers and volunteer to pack meals. www.fmsc.org

- **Way to Grow:** Volunteer to work with a minority low-income family so their children are ready for kindergarten. www.waytogrow.org

Faith based local and global missions:
- **CRU:** Volunteer to serve at faith-based events at a local college or university. www.cru.org

- **PULSE Movement:** Volunteer your time with this evangelistic ministry geared to the youth of America and the world. www.pulsemovement.com

- **Time to Revive:** Volunteer your time and talents at events and join with this evangelistic ministry to revive America. www.timetorevive.org

- **Shine in the World Ministries:** Volunteer your time on mission trips with this evangelistic ministry in Africa or with immigrants in Minnesota. www.shine intheworld.org

Micro finance and poverty alleviation:

- **HOPE International:** Participate in an Insight Trip to one of the sixteen countries where they offer micro financing to the poor. www.hopeinternational.org

- **Matter:** Volunteer to work in a warehouse categorizing donated items to local and global organizations to help the poor. www.mattermore.org

- **Opportunity International:** Participate in an Insight Trip to one of almost thirty countries where they offer micro financing to the poor. www.opportunity .org

Single moms:

- **Jeremiah Program:** Go with your friends or cowork-ers and cook a meal for single mothers and their children. www.jeremiahprogram.org

As mentioned above, there are countless ways to vol-unteer. You may have to volunteer working in an area that is not of your choosing but where the organization needs you most. In those times, you need to be patient and learn while you are there and wait for other opportu-nities to open up.

By serving on nonprofit boards and volunteering hands-on at several events and nonprofits, I learned how to serve on for-profit organization boards too. The re-wards I have received by serving are many, and each has significantly enriched my life. I have never considered it a waste of time. To the contrary, I consider my time in-vested an amazing opportunity to grow, learn, and meet remarkable people across the country (and the world). The time to volunteer is NOW. People need your help!

The same way you can discover additional talents by volunteering your time, you can also discover your em-ployees' additional talents that they don't necessarily use at your company. When you are in a position of leader-ship, you have a unique opportunity to develop your em-ployees' talents beyond their individual jobs by providing *them* with volunteer opportunities. These opportunities will not only expand their horizons, they will also build your own team. Volunteering together brings something special to people's hearts—coming together for one common cause. Your employees will appreciate these opportunities to serve together and also become more loyal to your company. In addition, your company may receive free publicity just because you chose to help the community with your team. The best way to do this is to take a small team and volunteer together during work hours, which means it's paid time.

I had the opportunity to help start the community involvement program at my last job. The executive team worked together to ensure we involved the entire staff in deciding which nonprofits we would help. We sent small teams of employees to volunteer together. We went to Feed My Starving Children, Matter, Jeremiah Program, and Youth Farm, for example. We mixed employees from various departments so they got to know each other, and everyone felt involved and appreciated. At the same time, employees grew as individuals, felt more fulfilled, and discovered new gifts and talents. Some of them even left banking to work at nonprofits. They found their purpose beyond their jobs. That is leading by maximizing talent! We talk more about maximizing the talents of those you lead in the next section.

Give shoes to the poor . . . it may be their only pair.
We may never understand poverty unless we walk in
others' shoes . . . Wait! They may not even have shoes!

Managing Your Time
Helps Maximize Your Talents

"Lost time is never found again."

—BENJAMIN FRANKLIN

We hear repeatedly that we all have the same number of hours in a day. We cannot stretch time. Time is set, and that is a fact we cannot change. If we don't learn to manage our time well, our lives become chaotic. We feel like we always have "unfinished business." We become unfulfilled individuals. We must learn to manage it, or we will live in a constant state of panic.

To begin, ask yourself some questions that may help you manage your time more effectively. For example, what type of atmosphere do you work best in? (i.e. fast pace, cutting-edge technology companies, group work, etc.) Are you having a challenge managing your time? Are you naturally an organized person? Do you struggle prioritizing your responsibilities in the various areas of your life? Once you know the answers to these questions, you can create a plan to improve in this area of your life. Here are some discoveries I came upon throughout my working life that may help you as well—especially if you are a new leader.

Job expectations. As a new leader in your organization, it is crucial to know the expectations of your job. Expectations can be in the form of deadlines and/or quality of products or services offered. Expectations can include measuring the development of those you lead, creating opportunities for them, and keeping them accountable. If your job is deadline-driven, you need to know what the deadlines are. Are those deadlines throughout the day? For example, in one of my previous banking jobs, I had to review business customers' accounts, pay down on their loans, or invest excess funds by 11:00 a.m. each day. If I missed that deadline, there were consequences such as the clients didn't earn interest on their accounts or were charged too much interest on their loans.

Is your job project-driven? If yes, you need to plan to meet your deadlines. Do you have project management skills and experience? If not, you need to learn what they are and acquire those skills. Hopefully, you work for a company that allows you to learn on the job as you go.

Remember, the higher you go in your leadership position, the less you will do and the more you will lead others.

Do you have regular meetings you need to attend? If yes, are they on your calendar for the entire year? Scheduling them in advance will avoid double-booking yourself in the future. All these are excellent questions to ask yourself so you can be successful as a leader.

Organizational skills. Having time management skills is closely related to having good organizational skills. Organization starts in your mind. Some people are more skilled at this than others. But it is a skill we can all improve on with practice. Often people spend a lot of time looking for things on their desks, and the same concept applies to an electronic work area. If you don't organize your electronic folders in a way that makes sense to you, you will *never* find documents when you need them. It may make you feel overwhelmed. The point I'm trying to make is: if your mind is cluttered, it will show in your work area. If you are an extremely organized and neat person, a messy work area can disturb your thoughts to the point of paralyzing you so you are not able to take action. Of course, there is a balance in everything. You need to find out how you work best and how you need to organize yourself to be the most effective and efficient possible using the talents you have.

Set your priorities in life. Life is busy enough just because it is. When you have a family and then add work and community involvement, your commitments could overtake you. Therefore it is necessary to have your priorities well-defined in your life. Only then will you be able to say "no" to activities and commitments that don't fall under one of your priorities. If you have children, it is also important to address the commitments and priorities of your children if you are their full-time driver. Agreeing together as a family on all the kids' commitments to sports, arts, or music is very important. You will not only help your children establish their own priorities, but the entire family can learn to respect each other's priorities and work together. By knowing your priorities, you will be able to utilize the same talents that you use at work also at home. Pastor Jared Van Voorst said it well, "I get to teach Bible studies at church and also get to do it as a dad."

When my kids were in school and didn't drive yet, I used to tell them, "Every commitment you make affects the entire family, so let's agree on what you want to get involved in before you commit." A couple of times, my husband and I had to ask them to choose between two sports that had conflicting schedules because driving them around was driving us crazy!

I always said, "Even the dog is affected by our commitments." Well, we didn't have a dog, but you get the point.

Equipment. Do you have the appropriate tools to do your job well? This includes the appropriate computer systems, calendars, and mobile devices that can assist you in managing your time. Even though some people may think that printing your calendar in addition to having it on your phone and your computer may be a waste of paper, for me it's an additional tool to help me stay organized and manage my time. I also color code my calendar based on the type of activity. At a glance I can see if my calendar is filled with business, personal, or community commitments. This helps me ensure I'm staying true to my priorities.

Hopefully you work for a company where technology and systems work well and consistently the way they're supposed to. There is nothing more frustrating for employees than having unreliable computers, systems that crash often, or reports produced from a system that are incorrect or not available. When computers work, everyone is happy—including your customers. When computers break for whatever reason, everyone in the company is crabby, irritable, and impatient. If you are in a leadership position, ensure your company invests in the best technology tools for your employees to do their jobs well.

Schedule everything—even free time. I learned through the years that I even have to schedule time I need to keep free. This includes time to work on a specific client project, time to develop a new presentation, and what I call "inspirational" time to write. If you don't protect your time by putting it in your calendar, you will fill it up with other activities. Of course, I have also learned to be more flexible with my schedule, but you can start by doing certain activities at specific times on a regular basis until they become a habit. For example, I do most of my inspirational writing on Saturdays. Sometimes you need to choose *not* to attend certain meetings. As Kevin Webb shared, "I don't attend meetings where I don't make a significant contribution." This is an important way to save time and only attend meetings where your contribution is truly needed as the leader of the team.

I take time to nurture my relationships as well and schedule coffee meetings even when I'm very busy. Meeting with people I love and care about not only refreshes me but feeds my soul. I come out inspired and excited to keep working. There are also times when I need to encourage my friends so they can walk away inspired and uplifted. The point is to make the time and schedule these important meetings on your calendar.

Manage your time in social media *wisely*. Even though social media has become part of our culture and daily workload, we need to wisely manage our time spent on LinkedIn, Facebook, Instagram, Twitter, and other media. Social media is important to the success of our businesses, but we need to be careful to not spend unnecessary time looking at things that only reduce our productivity.

Spending time choosing the right activities to become

involved in is crucial to staying focused and to managing time well. There is so much information available, it is impossible to keep up—even with the things that are relevant to your industry and/or your job. Therefore the other things, the "irrelevant" things, need to be set aside for the times when you truly need a distraction, a mindless activity to get refreshed so you can continue your work or family activity later. The point is to choose how you spend your time in your social media world wisely so the important things still get done.

Focus on one task at a time. It is now known and proven by various studies that our minds are not wired to multitask. So why do we insist in making our brains work so hard trying to multitask when we are not designed to do that? I now strive to focus on one activity at a time. Notice I said, I "strive" to focus on one thing at a time because, even though I try, the distractions are many. This means I only answer emails during a specific time of the day, but I'm flexible as to what time of the day that is based on what I have going on each day. I also only make phone calls during a specific time. As mentioned above, I write only one day a week instead of trying to sneak in an article here and there or trying to write one chapter on a book today and another at other times. It takes me at least twice the effort when I write that way versus when I'm in the "mode of writing." Some weeks, if I have the time, I add another writing day or an entire morning, also based on what I have going on the rest of the week.

I hope these ideas will help you improve your time management skills so you become a more productive and efficient leader. I recently heard a speaker say, "I don't believe in time management, because we all have the same amount of time, and it can't be managed."

Well I disagree. I believe we *can* manage our time if we want to. Otherwise, we will waste the most precious asset we possess—time. And we cannot ever have it back. However, even though we cannot add hours to our days, we can definitely produce more during the same amount of time if we improve our time management skills.

Managing and taking control of your time is one way to maximize your talents because you are choosing to spend time on your priorities, which include activities that develop your talents.

It takes time to find the right shoes.

PART II

DISCOVER AND MAXIMIZE THE TALENTS OF THOSE YOU LEAD

The Key to My Biggest Accomplishment as a Manager: Knowing My Employees

"I know in my heart that man is good. That what is right will eventually triumph. And there is purpose and worth to each and every life."

—RONALD REAGAN

As the end of each year approaches and a new year is about to begin, I find myself going through everything I did in the past year and making new goals for the next year. I usually ponder over my previous year's accomplishments and their significance. I ask myself, did I make a difference in the lives of others last year? Did I learn something new this past year?

When people ask me to share "my accomplishments in life," I surprise them with my response because it's not what they expect to hear. While accomplishments are usually measured by the successful companies you built, how many degrees you attained, or the titles you held at work, I don't consider my biggest accomplishment to be any of those.

One of my biggest accomplishments in life—and my biggest one as a manager—was that I never lost an employee because of a bad relationship with *me*. My secret? I get to know my employees as individuals. I encourage every leader and manager to do the same. Invest the time, nurture the relationships, and have high expectations of your employees. Believe in them and trust that they can do the job you hired them to do.

At the same time, I firmly believe in providing employees with the tools and training necessary to do the job. It is the company's responsibility to contribute to their success. If in the end, you do have to fire an employee because of incompetence, at least they will leave knowing that you cared about them. Those employees will leave with no hard feelings, which can protect the organization from potential lawsuits. Another thing to remember is, of course, to take all the steps according to the law and ensure proper documentation is completed prior to letting an employee go.

The first advice I give to new supervisors is, "Get to know your employees." But it's amazing to me to discover that leaders who have been in management positions for decades have never thought about this concept. They were taught and believed that you must have a clear line between work and outside life and they never bothered to get to know their staff.

Often, we hear and read in books the advice to not form personal relationships or friendships with our direct reports. I disagree. I strongly believe that when you get to know another person (in this case your employee) at the personal level, the relationship has the opportunity to flourish and be more successful. Of course, you, as the leader, need to be careful to not go too far into the relationship where it becomes inappropriate. You also must be able to maintain professionalism both inside and outside the workplace. You may be telling yourself right now that I'm contradicting myself, but let me explain. There is a balance between a friendship of an employee and boss (with professional boundaries) and other friendships that are completely outside of the workplace. It can be done, and it can be very successful.

Becoming friends with my employees is a rule that I break as a manager. I've had great success by establishing a friendship relationship with all my employees throughout my twenty-plus years of management. You simply need to establish clear boundaries of mutual respect and have very clear roles at work. You need to have the courage to discipline your employees when necessary as well as be able to praise them for a job well done. You need to be genuine and do both only when it truly matters. Otherwise, overdoing either discipline or praise may lose its effect.

One way to get to know your employees as individuals is to use the same tools with your employees that you use to get to know yourself. Employees will appreciate that you invest time and money in getting to know them. Dr. Bekele Shanko told me, "I take them through similar self-assessment tests, I observe the way they do things, have them discuss in a team environment about their talents and why they need one another to be effective in their leadership."

Employees are people—with feelings—not machines with the sole purpose of producing and increasing company profitability. When you take care of your employees and get to know them at the personal level, the rest comes by itself. They will perform consistently beyond your expectations. I have very high expectations for myself and for those who work for me. I strive for excellence at every level and try to be an example to my employees in everything I do, so I can expect the same of them. And they follow. Because my employees know that I care for them and their families, they don't want to let me down.

Pastor Jared Van Voorst discovers his employees' talents by "taking time to build relationships first and not seeing them as a means to an end."

During my years in management, I have laid off employees, fired a few for non-performance, and promoted all my employees at some point. I remember when I was the director of HR, I had to lay off an employee who was very nice, but the position was eliminated. When the staff found out about the layoff, and because they knew how much I cared for the employee, they felt sadder for me having to do the difficult job of laying the employee off than the employee who was being laid off! They knew I was hurting for that person. The separation went extremely well, and there were no hard feelings. The same situation happened again when I had to fire an employee for not performing the job well. I was so sad to have to do it but had to because it was the best for the organization (and eventually for the employee too). Sometimes people forget that Human Resources professionals have feelings too and really do care about people.

Several studies have demonstrated that pay is not the top reason employees leave a company. It is because of their boss. A bad boss, a micro-manager, or a controlling or insecure boss can be devastating to the employees they manage. Simply put, a bad boss is misery for anyone, so you must ensure you are not one of them. Being aware of your own tendencies and faults is the best thing you can do to avoid these situations. As I shared in Part I, knowing yourself is crucial to be a successful manager and to hold any position of leadership.

In addition to creating a negative environment for employees who work for a bad boss, the company will experience a high level of turnover, which is costly for the organization. Companies spend millions of dollars every year training new employees. The Human Resources staff spends most of their time *hiring* new people instead of *developing* the current employees and investing in them. In addition, high turnover issues can become public due to disgruntled employees sharing on their social media pages about their experiences. This creates reputational risk for the companies they worked for.

One way that Gene Cross discovers his employees' talents is by "letting them grow and not boxing them in." He shared, "Allow them to do things their way. You work with them and help them succeed. Allow them to fail and help them get up. I love seeing my employees succeed and then I make sure they get the appropriate credit by becoming their advocate within the organization."

Another great way to discover your individual employees' talents is through the performance review process. Ask them where they see themselves in the next three to five years and also what their ultimate career goal is. Ask them what other activities or tasks they would like to perform in the company that is currently outside of the scope of their individual jobs. This question can reveal other talents they're not using in their current job. Ask them what they aspire to be and what they believe are pieces missing in their credentials or experience in order to get there. I have heard of many stories where an employee leaves an organization to go acquire a specific skill and then comes back to perform the job he or she was aspiring to do. When employees know that your company cares about them as individuals, they will come back— and bring even more value than when they first started working for your company. This time they will be more committed and loyal to your organization.

Once you know your employees better, as opportunities present themselves to give them different or new tasks, you'll know which employee is the most capable to do that particular task. When you do this with each employee over time, they will know that you have the best intentions at heart. They will come looking for additional opportunities to grow. Keep in mind that you need to be okay if they fail at the new task. By trying new things, employees learn what they like or don't like doing. They also learn what they are really good at and what they're not naturally good at. The ideal situation is when they find something they like doing *and* they're naturally good at it.

As covered previously, an excellent way to discover your employees' individual talents is by offering them opportunities to volunteer outside of work. Beyond knowing their strengths and personality, you need to get to know their heart. What causes are they passionate about? Who do they like to help? What types of activities fire them up and make them excited? Often employees decide to dedicate their free time for a cause. Have them organize a fundraising activity and help them achieve their fundraising goals as well as encourage others to participate. These are great opportunities for them to demonstrate leadership outside of work and promote team building and friendships in the workplace. Kevin Webb gets to know his employees by "engaging with them and spending time with them."

If you're thinking, *Wow, this is a lot of work*! or *When am I going to have time to get to know each person and tailor to their individual needs for growth?* then management may not be for you. Doing these things is easy when you have the "gift" of leadership and the desire to see those you lead succeed—in every area of their lives—not only in the workplace. The satisfaction you will receive as a leader when you discover and maximize your employees' talents is priceless, and it is definitely worth the investment of your time.

I once worked with a division manager who told me that "the *opportunity cost* of me visiting with my direct reports is too high compared to the business I could bring in." *Wow!* I thought to myself, *You absolutely should not be in a management position. You are not a leader!* But I simply walked away and said nothing, feeling sure that this person would not have taken such feedback well. But in the meantime, the employees did not feel valued by their boss and they were hurt. Years later, I heard this person was no longer in management.

Knowing your employees at the personal level means you know their talents, you know their personalities, you learn about their families, and you connect at some personal level. They know you care about them. It means that you open new doors for them to allow them the chance to grow and learn new things beyond the scope of their daily jobs. The result is a culture with loyal employees who know you value them. They can now focus on excelling at their jobs so you can give them yet new opportunities. Even the employees who don't have as much ambition will feel valued and, at least, will likely perform beyond what they thought they could. Why? Because you believed in them enough to get to know them as a person. They will feel appreciated. And they will go the extra mile for you as their leader and for your organization.

Jen Ford Reedy asks, "How do you create a truly supportive and high performing culture?" As a leader, her answer was to create a culture with clear operating values, that get expectations for what employees expect of each other. "The values are at the core of the culture. They are how we hold ourselves accountable to each other and to our mission."

Enjoy being a manager. You have a tremendous opportunity to influence your employees' lives in a positive way. Take advantage of that opportunity and develop your employees. Train them and give them career opportunities. Brainstorm with them about what else they would like to do and promote them if you have the power to do so. Invest time in building relationships with your employees. It will pay off. Understanding that not everyone wants to be your friend, your employees can at least know you are interested in them. Most will reciprocate, and doing so will help you discover their individual talents.

As you can see, knowing yourself and discovering your own talents helps you become an influential and impactful leader. The same way, knowing your employees helps you discover their talents and allows you the opportunity to help them grow—and this is all part of being a successful leader. Getting to know your team takes time, discipline, patience, and dedication on your part as the leader. But it definitely pays off many times over. When you invest your own time in your employees, they will follow you and work with you to accomplish the vision of the company.

*Sometimes the biggest accomplishment in a day
is to choose the right shoes.*

Mentoring Changes Lives

"Anything done for another is done for oneself."

—POPE JOHN PAUL II

believe in mentoring. Mentoring is powerful because it truly changes people's lives. You want to make a difference? You want to impact someone's life? You want to influence someone? You want to leave a legacy? Mentor someone. In this chapter, I focus on you as the "mentor" as part of being a leader.

The word *mentor* means trusted counselor or guide, tutor, or coach, and it became synonymous with trusted advisor, friend, teacher, and wise person. Over the years, I have read a lot about mentoring. I have been a mentor, and I have been a mentee. I have learned some things about mentoring that helped me that may also help you as a leader.

Mentoring can start from a small conversation with a friend or it can be formally decided between two individuals. It can be set up by company leadership or be informally done between two colleagues in the workplace. Mentoring is about teaching others, imparting to others, and sharing useful information about what you have learned during your life. You can help your mentee avoid making the same mistakes you made, or simply do things better or improve in those areas.

Mentoring is helping others be successful in their lives, knowing that you are one of the reasons they *can* and *will* do many things. Mentoring is providing the right advice at the right time with the information you currently have. Mentoring is knowing when to stop helping your mentee and recognize when your job as mentor is done. The job of a mentor may only be for a season or in a specific area of the mentee's life.

As a manager, you have a unique opportunity to mentor your employees in many ways. By doing so, you can help them discover their talents and gain ideas on how to develop those talents. You can mentor them on how to succeed in their specific jobs, how to continue to grow in their careers, and how to navigate the political environment in the company (most companies have some politics whether we like it or not).

Gene Cross shared, "It's really rewarding to mentor a young person and give them more complex loan deals to think about. Allow them to give their opinion first, then mentor them about other important aspects of a deal that they may not have considered. Giving them increasing levels of responsibility is very rewarding."

As you mature in your career, and if you achieve an executive leadership position, you have the unique opportunity to mentor other leaders and managers on your team. You can mentor them to become more effective managers and, in certain cases, even help them decide if they should stay in leadership or move back to performing a non-management job.

In both cases, and as stated in the previous chapter, getting to know your employees—whether they themselves are in leadership positions or not—is key to your success as a mentor. The more you know your employees, the better you can mentor them. When you mentor someone, you are accomplishing three major things: 1) You get to know yourself as a mentor. 2) You discover whether you even like mentoring. 3) You start discovering your employees' natural abilities. This knowledge is very valuable as you learn to lead and drive results by maximizing talent this way. I should add here that not all managers mentor their employees but most leaders naturally mentor their employees, those they lead.

I started mentoring others as I matured in my career.

Several young men and women asked me to mentor them because they saw me as a role model and wanted me to help them be successful. While it is an honor to be considered a role model, it is an enormous responsibility to be someone's mentor, because he or she has high expectations of you as the mentor.

Choosing a mentor and becoming one should be a carefully thought-out process. It's the responsibility of the mentor to provide the right advice at the right time *and only when asked*. When the mentee takes the mentor seriously and is committed to succeed, he or she will follow the mentor's advice. Jeanne Crain, president and CEO of Bremer Financial Corporation, recommends new leaders to, "Find a role model. Don't expect leadership to be intuitive. Make sure you find someone to watch that supports you—a mentor."

In a healthy mentoring relationship, the mentee needs to learn to think independently and not ask for advice about every little decision. Similarly, the mentor should not be controlling so that the mentee cannot make a decision without the mentor's approval. The mentor needs to know the mentee will make decisions without consulting them first and respect the mentee for that, even if the mentor disagrees with the decision. The mentor needs to work with the mentee after he or she made a poor decision without criticizing or judging.

A mentor has to be open and willing to help others.

Sometimes the person you want to stay away from, the negative employee in the workplace, is the one who needs the most help. You may need to reach out to that person. When you open your heart to help someone, the gift of compassion is in you and the opportunity for mentoring happens. The other person may open up as well, and a successful mentoring relationship can begin. Not every mentor relationship will be successful, but if you follow the simple suggestions in this chapter, you have a much better chance to succeed as a mentor and make an impact on someone's life forever.

Throughout your life, stay open to the idea of mentoring someone. Mentoring relationships are some of the most fulfilling relationships you can have because you see the fruit of your work, the positive influence you can have in others, and how your talents can help others succeed. Melissa Johnston believes in mentoring too. She says, "My mentor has been extremely helpful in providing ways for me to maintain my confidence, leadership, and focus in a male-dominated industry. My mentor encouraged me to take on as many interesting special projects as my schedule allowed. Coordinating, facilitating, and leading a variety of task forces over the years has been instrumental in nurturing my leadership skills. As the bank continues to adapt to a changing marketplace, we continue to roll out new project teams that I often lead."

I have mentors who, throughout my life helped me in

my personal life, spiritual life, and in my career. I have also mentored over fifteen young adults during high school, their college years, and while entering the workforce. I helped them with interviewing skills, preparing their resumes, negotiating salaries, getting promotions, connecting them to potential employers, and coaching them through work situations once employed. I have also mentored more seasoned adults going through transitions at work or switching careers. The little help I provided impacted their lives in various ways and for a long time.

Because I strongly believe in mentoring, I volunteered to be on the Board of Big Brothers Big Sisters of the Greater Twin Cities (BBBSGTC). During the six years I served, I was involved in the Finance Committee, then served in the Executive Committee, and lastly as the board chair for two years. Those years were a valuable experience as I witnessed how mentoring changes lives. The nonprofit organizations that track results of mentoring relationships show that children who are mentored have a much higher percentage chance of graduating from high school and over 80% of those children aspire for higher level education.

If you don't desire to or have the time to be in a formal mentoring program, then do it informally. But mentor someone! Most people need a little coaching from time to time. It is the best way to give back to the younger generation and pass on your own hard-earned wisdom.

Mentoring is a way to show young men and women that they are valuable, and that they too can make a difference in the world.

As leaders, we need to impart to the younger generation what we have learned during our lives and help them prepare to succeed in the working environment. If you are in a leadership position, you probably have opportunities to mentor others. Some of the main traits that good mentors possess are self-confidence, maturity, generosity, and humility. I encourage you to reach out and mentor someone who is willing to hear your advice. You will expand your leadership skills and help that person discover his or her talents. You will have opportunities to open doors for that person in places that may otherwise be out of his or her reach, both inside your organization as well as outside.

A mentor is like having shoes . . . everyone needs them.

Reverse Mentoring: Do You Need It?

*"To add value to others,
one must first value others."*

—John Maxwell

Continuing on the subject of mentoring, a couple of years ago I heard the term "reverse mentoring" for the first time, and it caught my attention. We all know what the usual "mentoring" means—usually an older, wiser, and more mature person advises a younger or less-experienced person. So what is reverse mentoring? As the word *reverse* implies, it's the other way around. In this case, a young person mentors an older person. And why would we need reverse mentoring in the workplace?

I'll answer that with another question. What might the younger generation know better than the older generations? Technology!

We often associate wisdom with age, but wisdom has no age. It's true that we acquire wisdom through the years. But we also know people who are way older than us who are unwise or display a complete lack of wisdom. That's when a younger person can be wiser than an older person—especially when we talk about technology and how to use it successfully and wisely.

When I coach older employees and my Baby Boomer friends regarding the workplace, I always suggest two key things in order for them to be and stay successful in the current business environment. First, I encourage them to learn new technology *and* stay current with all the changes. Secondly, I recommend they maintain an open-minded attitude as they learn new technology and keep learning it.

Learning new things takes time and effort. For older generations to succeed and have an impact in their later work years, they need to learn new technologies to perform their jobs well. The problem is, technology changes continually. So all workers must continue the learning journey. For younger workers, learning new technology is easier because it's what they're used to. They were given their first cellphone almost as soon as they could hold a bottle! For them, new software or a new gadget is fun. It's a new adventure, something to conquer, and is used immediately in their jobs—like conquering the next level in a video game. This situation creates a huge advantage for younger workers over those from older generations who grew up without using much technology. But this shouldn't be the end of the world for the older workers. It's not that they're less smart. The solution is simply to have a good attitude and an open mind to learn the new technology—continually. The more the brain gets used to the "exercise of learning," the easier it is to continue to learn. The best way to exercise the brain is, precisely, to learn. Just as your body needs the physical exercise to stay fit, your brain needs to continue learning so it can expand and stay fruitful and productive during the later years.

If you are a new leader, and a young leader, you may find opportunities to mentor those in the older generations who need help with technology in addition to mentoring the generation coming after you. A young mentor will feel valuable and appreciated, and the older mentee will feel smarter and more valuable as well. For both sides, it will take patience, a positive attitude, and knowing that you are both on the same team.

A favorite story I like to share about reverse mentoring is from one of my previous jobs. My boss was the "older" worker, and my employee, the director of IT, was the "younger" worker. My boss didn't know how to create folders within Outlook to keep the important emails he wanted or needed to store for later use. As a result, he kept deleting them. Then he asked the director of IT to train him—again—on how to retrieve his emails once lost. This situation continued to occur so often that both parties were frustrated with each other.

I saw an opportunity for mentoring and talked with each of them. I asked my boss to please be patient with technology, to change his attitude toward it, and truly try to learn how to use Outlook the proper way. Otherwise, I assured him, "you will frustrate the younger workers." Then I talked with my employee and told him to be patient with the president and give him extra grace. After all, I needed the president's approval to promote this person in the future.

We scheduled formal training sessions for the two of them together. Months passed and they started forming a friendship. They both changed their attitudes toward each other and toward technology. A year later, they had become such great friends that when the younger worker got married, the older worker was his best man! If that's not the best story of reverse mentoring, I don't know what is.

Reverse mentoring may also have a positive impact on the business profitability as older workers can potentially become more efficient. Knowing and continuing to learn technology is not only for IT people. Technology is for everyone, regardless of age.

Old shoes may be comfortable,
but new ones are shinier. We need both.

Effective Strategies For
Succession Planning
at All Levels

"Lead me, follow me, or get out of my way."

—George S. Patton

When we think of succession planning, we immediately think of the CEO and/or president of a company and perhaps the senior leadership positions in an organization. This group may or may not include you at this point in your leadership career, but it's important for you to be aware of succession-planning strategies. Having a successor for the top positions is crucial to have in place. At a minimum, the board of directors should have documented discussions about succession plans. From the talent management perspective (which should include maximizing your entire staff's talents) and also from the risk management perspective, it is wise to think of the entire company as a whole regarding succession planning.

Small businesses don't have the luxury of having depth of staff, meaning there is only one person performing one type of role. In addition, that one person ends up wearing several hats—sometimes too many. One could argue that it is a great opportunity for employees because they get to learn about the various areas of the organization, which makes them more marketable. From the risk perspective however, this situation presents a challenge for small companies if a key employee leaves, is promoted to another position, or simply goes on vacation for a week, and there is no successor.

The topic of succession planning falls under various areas within organizations. Succession planning is part of talent management (Human Resources), which entails assessing the talent of the organization to see if there are internal candidates to potentially fill key positions within the company. Talent management should be integrated into the overall organization's strategic plan so the company can clearly see the type of talent needed in the future and develop strategies to attract and retain that talent.

At the same time, succession planning is critical to the overall enterprise's risk management. If the company's leader is no longer there, the organization must have a plan to implement immediately. I call it a "disaster recovery plan for the CEO." But what about the other crucial positions in the organization such as the operations person who has been with the company for thirty years? What about the employee who knows how everything is done and holds an immense amount of knowledge in his or her head? Who will do their jobs when they move on—whether that's unexpectedly or planned? What about the middle managers? As a new leader, do you have a plan for your own successor?

It is important to the success and future of any organization and, in your case as a leader, for the department or division you lead, to have a succession plan for every position—from the top senior level to entry-level positions. Where do you start? I always start from the talent management approach. First, identify all key positions throughout the organization—regardless of title. Then create a backup plan for all the critical positions of the company (at every level). This backup plan includes cross-training employees and establishing procedures that anyone can follow. Having backup and cross-training are two strategies that avoid a crisis in unexpected situations and also for planned vacations, so the company operations continue to run smoothly when key employees are out. The next step is to *write* a succession plan for all critical positions, and make it part of your strategic plan.

Your position as a leader is one of those critical positions.

Let's look at succession planning from the perspective of maximizing your employees' individual talents. How do you maximize each person's talents? One way is by providing cross-training and backup opportunities to all employees. These two steps will help your employees grow and learn something new. At the same time, you will be creating a succession plan that will feel natural for everyone. Now every time a key employee goes on vacation, you have automatic backup already trained and ready to perform. If that key person decides to leave, you have your internal replacement right there.

Remember to also have your key people be backup for others. They all need to continue to learn and grow in different areas. The trick is to do it with every employee as a matter of best practice across the organization. When you do it as a best practice, you will avoid employees feeling threatened about losing their jobs.

As you put the cross-training plan in place, you will discover that some people may actually fit better in another position, more than the incumbent. Other times, the employees themselves will discover that the new tasks they're backing up are more enjoyable. They may ask you to be moved permanently. These challenges may happen naturally and you'll need to choose wisely as to whom to put in what places. Having the right people in the right places is part of the talent management program in your organization. Succession planning is at the core of a well-thought-out talent management program, and it will benefit your organization now and in the future.

Greg Shamey described how he maximized his employees' individual talents during his first management job where he oversaw a team in another country with a different culture, "How do you develop those relationships and work through biases and assumed behaviors? I assumed the best and started meeting via video conferencing, and I started to get to know the team members. This created a great cohesiveness." He then asked himself, *Why can't this team perform some of the more complex tasks?* "I gave them permission to challenge and question why we were doing certain functions. This gave the remote team the opportunity to maximize their talents and improve processes."

Creating cross-training opportunities, establishing backups for all positions, and allowing your employees to challenge the existing processes are all effective strategies for you to maximize your employees' talents while implementing a succession plan at all levels.

When you put on your own shoes
and start walking, others will follow.

Hiring Young Talent and Maximizing Their Talents

"The future starts today, not tomorrow."

—POPE JOHN PAUL II

One major challenge that companies face more often is the ongoing question of how to attract and retain "young" talent. However, when your company is known as a company that helps to discover and maximize their employees' talents, attracting young talent will not be an issue. Younger workers are desperately looking for companies to value their gifts and help them—genuinely help them—develop those unique talents. Once you are able to attract young talent and help them develop their gifts, you will not have a problem retaining them. Why?

Because just like any other worker, they want to feel valued and appreciated. Helping young workers discover their natural abilities and supporting them by providing opportunities to develop those abilities, creates loyalty. They will not want to leave your company. In fact, they will tell their friends about your company, and you will attract even more young talent.

My question to you as a leader is, are you ready to take in these young workers who are eager to start their careers? Are you willing to help them find their way and teach them to navigate the business environment? Dr. Bekele Shanko offered, "One of the ways is to allow each employee to operate from his or her area of strength, but continually increase their responsibilities so that they are growing and maximizing their talents."

In addition to a college degree or technical certification on a specific trade, young leaders need other soft skills in order to be successful in the workplace. There are several elements that an employer looks for in a candidate, and several things a candidate can do to rise to the top of the list. Most employers look for the *whole package*—a person who has the credentials plus the soft skills to do the job.

If you are a young leader, these are some of the critical soft skills you must possess and develop in order to accelerate your success in the business world. If you are a more seasoned worker in a new leadership position and you want to attract and retain young talent, provide young workers with opportunities to develop and grow in these areas. Developing soft skills allows employees to grow as leaders and develop their unique talents simultaneously.

Sociability. This skill includes networking, friendliness, a genuine interest in getting to know other people, a good/clean sense of humor, and being a connector of people. Networking and knowing people are still essential for getting employed and growing in your career once employed. Sometimes it may take up to the third of fourth circle of referrals or connections until something works out. Persevering is key to success. The more connections you make and follow up on, the more opportunities open up. As a leader, you can provide networking opportunities to young workers by inviting them to social events.

Presence. This is the representation of the total person as a complete package. It includes your appearance, which in turn includes grooming, stance, handshake, clothing, and your entire presence that creates that first impression. Exercising is crucial to staying in shape, which is part of your presence. As a leader, provide opportunities to young workers to improve their presence. This could be included in a mentoring program or by providing access to a gym or even hiring a personal coach or personal stylist.

Presentation. Part of your presence is your presentation and public speaking skills, which include one-on-one meetings, small or large group presentations, and phone and online live interviews or meetings. Many companies are now interviewing candidates via video/online platforms. Remember to be yourself during these meetings as that is crucial for people to go to the next step as a candidate for a job or to like you as a presenter (if you're giving a presentation). In addition, practicing and preparing are foundational to help you feel self-confident and thus to deliver a strong, successful presentation.

When I was in sales, my boss sent me to a professional public speaking seminar where they filmed me five times behind a clear podium. Part of the training was to make an impromptu presentation on any random topic and also to present a topic I had a little time to prepare for. I was critiqued and received amazing feedback that helped me improve as a speaker and presenter. As a leader, don't be afraid to invest in young workers who have potential to make your company look good in front of stakeholders. Even when people have natural gifts, you can provide opportunities to develop those talents and make them superb at what they do.

Attitude. Your attitude every day is a reflection of your heart. Your mood, how you feel about yourself and about life, your tone of voice, and your behavior all show up on your face. As part of your preparation before important meetings and presentations, think of positive experiences, think of the people you love and who love you, think of places that relax you and give you peace.

Your attitude is reflected on how you treat others—including your employees, peers, and the top leaders in the organization. Assume the senior leadership of your company is always watching you, not necessarily to catch you doing something wrong. On the contrary, they are watching for potential future senior leaders of the company.

As a leader, your attitude is a reflection of your leadership and affects the entire company. Your attitude reflects your appreciation (or lack of) for your employees. Your attitude shows if you love your job in the company or if you're in the wrong place. Your attitude reflects whether you trust your employees. Your employees—of every age—are watching your every move. Often your attitude and actions determine whether employees will stick around or look for another job elsewhere. Again, they want to bring their talents where they feel appreciated. A great goal to have as a leader is for your employees to want to imitate your character. You are their example. Your employees will treat each other, as well as all your constituencies, the same way you treat them. They observe how you treat everyone involved in the business.

Enthusiasm. Leaders show enthusiasm. If you're not the type of person who shows enthusiasm and excitement about anything because that's your personality, that's okay—most of the time.

Your enthusiasm about your company, products, or

services will be infectious to your employees. If you're an introvert or don't show emotions as much as others because of your personality, still make an effort to express enthusiasm for everything you do. You will see a change in your employees' enthusiasm and their attitudes. Being an introvert is not a negative. It's simply your personality and that is okay.

Delegation. You must learn to delegate—even the things you love doing. That's the only way you will grow as a leader. Delegation is not a talent. It's a skill you can get better at every day by practicing. Pastor Jared Van Voorst encourages leaders to "provide opportunities and empower your employees to do things they're not required to do—delegate to them when you know they can do it. To know they're trusted is enough for them to do it."

Values. We often hear the question, "Do you have the right people?" As mentioned in a previous chapter, the "right people" are those who share your company values. Therefore, it is imperative that you have clarity in your company's values and that you, as the leader, share them often with all your employees.

As a leader in your organization, hire the right employees for your company, those who share your values and whose skills and talents fit your company's needs. It is better to find workers whose values align with your company's than to hire talented people whose values are not a match with your company's values. The first step is to hire the right *talent* (the person) who also possesses the right *talents*. Then you put that person in the right place and start developing his or her talents—that's how you maximize the talents of those you lead.

Jen Ford Reedy's advice to new leaders is to "Learn how to manage up and out. It should not be seen as a negative. Ask yourself these questions: What do you know that others could use? and What do others know that could help you? What effect are you having in the rest of the organization?"

Aleesha Webb shared her advice to her younger self, "Be me. Who I am is good enough. Although every experience is invaluable, feeling comfortable in your own skin is really a superpower." And I would add that, feeling comfortable in *your shoes* is a superpower!

When I asked Aleesha what leadership qualities organizations are looking for, she replied, "Accountability, laser focus, curiosity, and creative and critical thinking. Curiosity makes sure we never stop thinking, *What's next?*"

As children, we all start wearing little shoes and fit into bigger sizes as we develop and grow.

Do You Allow Your Employees to Flourish?

"It is neither wealth nor splendor, but tranquility and occupation which give happiness."

—THOMAS JEFFERSON

In Part I, we discussed how you, as an employee, can flourish in your work environment. Now put yourself on the other side of the equation. Do you allow your employees to explore and expand their talents? When employees work in a job where they can utilize their talents, they grow, have less anxiety, and produce more. The company maximizes their employees' strengths. The following are strategies you can use as a manager and leader to create a growth environment for your employees:

Trust that your employees can do their jobs. That's why you hired them in the first place. Micromanaging your employees will only create anxiety, and you will eventually lose them. No one likes to be micromanaged. I used to tell my employees that I trusted them in two ways. First, I trusted that they were good people, trustworthy employees who were there to earn an honest living. Second, I trusted they could do the job I hired them to do. I trusted their skills and knew they had the talent to perform the duties of the job. I provided them with guidelines and, depending on the project or nature of the job, I provided them with specific instructions. Then I left them alone to go do it.

Kevin Webb advises, "Give your employees opportunities but also get out of their way. If you're micromanaging people, you hired wrong. I spend little time with employees who are performing well."

I was careful not to dump work on my employees and instead delegated the appropriate tasks and provided direction. I also gave them the opportunity to come back with questions. Some of them came back several times, and sometimes I figured out I had not given them clear direction. Others didn't come back at all and a couple of days later showed up with exactly what I asked them to do. If it was a report, it may not have been the color or format I had in my head, but I got the results I needed. Many times, the results were better than if I had given them every step of the project.

Challenge your employees with new things where they can use other talents they may not have an opportunity to use in their daily work. Doing so re-energizes them and encourages them to continue to grow. They will appreciate that you think of them beyond their job and develop as a person too.

One good example of this was when we developed the first community involvement program. We formed a team of volunteer staff and assigned responsibilities for the various goals we set out to do. The community involvement program was not part of anyone's job responsibilities, but we knew we wanted to make a difference as an organization.

Those who volunteered in this committee reaped the rewards of serving. They led various events, met some of the community leaders that led the nonprofits, and gained visibility within the organization, including with the board of directors. After several years of serving in this committee, one of the employees now works as the executive director for one of the nonprofits we supported! That story is one of the best success stories of reaping the rewards when you volunteer to do something beyond the scope of your job.

One of my favorite stories from my leaders' interviews is from Heidi Gesell. As she got to know one of her employees who was leading the Loan Servicing Department, she discovered that this person would be a good fit for a Human Resources role her bank was creating. She encouraged the employee to take the opportunity even though the employee had not thought about it. The employee took the chance and has been their head of HR for the past fifteen years.

Gene Cross shared another story of when he promoted an administrative assistant. "She came to my office repeatedly with new ways of doing things that were far more efficient than how we did them at the time we were currently doing them. I asked her to join the credit team as a credit analyst, and that became her new career where she excels at concise, efficient write-ups." These are great success stories of how allowing employees to flourish can be a win-win for both the employee and the company.

Value your employees and acknowledge their talents and what they bring to your organization as a person. Get to know their hobbies and other interests. Create an environment where they can grow and flourish. When you provide additional opportunities to grow, their loyalty toward you and toward the company will significantly increase. Even when employees don't like their jobs very much, they now have a new reason to stay—new learning opportunities.

As employees are re-energized by learning new things, they become motivated to continue learning which in turn makes them more productive. They can't wait to finish their routine work so they can get to the "fun stuff" and the *new* responsibilities.

Nichol Beckstrand described how she values her employees, "I have always valued humble leaders. I think that is because I am much more likely to give praise to someone when they are not constantly seeking praise. My experience has also taught me that compassion is necessary. You can be driven and expect high performance, but when life happens you need to show compassion first."

When you value your employees, you will notice that errors decrease because employees' loyalty increases and they don't want to disappoint you as their manager. They want to succeed with the new duties and projects because they feel you trusted them with something different beyond their regular job. They feel special. At the same time, when you allow them the opportunity to make mistakes because they are human, you are creating a non-threatening culture where employees feel safe to grow and explore.

Pastor Jared Van Voorst talked about a success story when he valued and recognized one of his employees who had a gift for teaching but was in a different job at the time. Pastor Jared created an opportunity for this employee to serve as a teacher/pastor for the youth group and, since then, the employee moved to that position full-time. The employee flourished in his new position and impacted many youths as a result of this change.

Lastly, when you provide opportunities for your employees to flourish you will notice their attitude will improve and they will be more positive. Employees like to be trusted and want to feel valued. As a manager and leader, you will enjoy the results. You will feel so much more fulfilled and you will reap the rewards. I know I have.

Allow your employees to sometimes wear the wrong shoes.

A New Concept:
Invest Your Time

"If you judge people,
you have no time to love them."

—MOTHER TERESA

In this chapter, I want to introduce you to the concept of *investing* your time. Besides *managing* your time effectively and efficiently as discussed previously, when it comes to people, you need to *invest* your time in them. But you may be asking yourself these questions: What about all the other responsibilities I carry in my daily life? How am I going to carve additional time out of my overwhelmingly busy schedule to spend with the people I love? How can I dedicate more quality time to my employees when the business calls for my attention with never-ending urgent matters?

There is a way: by *investing* your time wisely.

The people we care about want and need more of our time *always*. Time is the best gift we can give to our families and our employees anytime through the year, not just during the holidays. Therefore, change your perspective on how you view time. Instead of thinking you are *using* your time for activities, people, business, work, or volunteering, think of the concept of *investing* your time. I learned this concept in "The Master's Program for Women" that I teach.[2] The analogy is to think of time as money and your investment portfolio as the places you choose to invest your time. Just as you invest your money in various types of ventures, you can invest your time in various types of activities (your portfolio). Again, just as you need to diversify your money portfolio you need to diversify your time portfolio. Similarly, you need to choose the best investment vehicles for your money to grow and not waste it, you also need to choose the best ways to spend, or invest, your time so you produce the most you can and not waste any of it. Here are some suggestions to help you invest your time more wisely where it matters most—in people.

---

2   Visit www.themastersprogramforwomen.org to learn more about TMPW.

Choose the right investment vehicles for your time.
Always start with people. Invest your time in *relationships,* and prioritize your days based on the circumstances and the urgency of the situation. As a manager and leader, you need to spend time with your boss, your coworkers, employees, vendors, customers, and other stakeholders. I have coached several individuals who became the president of the organization without any previous management or supervisory experience. If this is your case and you are now the "the boss," you need to invest quality time with the board of directors and shareholders or owners of the company—in addition to investing time with your employees.

Next, choose the *activities* that will produce the most results in your life. You need to invest a significant amount of time in your work. But that needs to be done wisely. If you don't set boundaries, your work will most likely take over other areas of your life. Lastly, choose volunteer activities where you are most fulfilled and, again, where your time investment will produce the most return (reward). If you know yourself well and discovered your talents (as discussed in Part I), choosing the right time investment as a volunteer will be much easier.

Be present at home. When you set aside time to be with your children, be present. Give them quality time, your undivided attention, and they will be satisfied and go on to do other activities once their time with you is done. I did this when my children were growing up and gave them an hour each afternoon to do whatever they wanted to do with me. Some days they chose to play a game, other days they wanted to play outside or go to the park. Yet other times, they decided to watch a movie or read books. I noticed that after the one-hour dedicated time I gave them, they actually left me. They went off to do their homework or play on their own. Many times, we are with them physically but not present. And kids know it. They sense when your mind is somewhere else and when you're not interested in the game or whatever activity you're doing with them. In the summers, for many years, I took an entire week to do whatever my kids wanted to do (usually, we visited swimming pools around the city or had picnics). Those are the memories they still have of "kids and mama." My husband had less vacation than I did during those years, so this was my dedicated time with the kids. As a full-time working mom, this decision to spend that dedicated time with my children helped create some of the best memories we now cherish.

If you are married, do the same with your spouse. Your spouse needs dedicated time when he or she is the center of your universe. Choose to do activities that you both enjoy and be present for him or her. I have found that when the kids were growing up, we needed to schedule our time together and plan ahead. For example, for several years we had lunch together every Friday until our work situation changed and we could no longer do that. Now that our kids are grown, we have the luxury to do impromptu things like going to a movie or to the park.

As a leader, encourage your employees to spend quality time with their families. Sometimes it's not the kids that need them anymore because they are grown or live somewhere else. It could be their parents or grandparents that need your employees to take them to doctor appointments or to simply spend quality time with them.

The key message is to be present with the person you're with at the time and be purposeful in investing your time with your family. When things are going well at home and in your personal life, you will be more productive at work.

Be present at work. When you schedule time to be with your employees, be present. Make sure they know this is their special time with you where they have your undivided attention. To prepare for the weekly meeting with my direct reports, we both wrote down the things we needed to talk about that were not urgent and that was our informal agenda for the meeting. We met more often if we were working on special projects or time sensitive issues. What I discovered was that since they knew they had one hour a week dedicated to them, they rarely interrupted me during the week. Of course, I was available for the important, urgent, or unexpected issues. But as time went by, urgent matters didn't come up as often because we planned together during our meetings. Consistency is key to having successful relationships with your employees. You can apply this same concept when you are meeting with your boss, clients, directors, or vendors.

When I asked Kevin Webb how he helps his employees maximize their talents, he said that by spending time with his employees, he finds out what their goals are—income goals, flexible schedule, and personal goals. "I manage people differently based on their personalities and personal goals too."

Be strategic on how you invest your time at work. I have found that the best way to manage my time in the office is to be strategic as to where I invest my time daily, as well as planning ahead. Be strategic on how you plan group meetings. Invite the right people, use and follow an agenda, start and end on time—consistently. Being consistent on how you run your meetings gives you credibility because you send the message that you value people's time.

Another way to invest your time wisely is to plan projects ahead to avoid a last-minute crisis. This is a no-brainer, but I'm sure you know countless people who wait until the last minute to prepare their part of a project or come to a meeting completely unprepared. They are sending a message to the rest of the team that their time is more valuable than the team's. At the same time, the other team members are evaluating to see if they should invest their time in that person's project. As a leader, do not procrastinate as this will only create chaos, and your employees and/or peers will lose respect for you. Nobody likes to put out fires all the time. Let the fires be the real, unexpected situations. Let them be the exception.

I encourage you to view the concept of time differently so you can start implementing these suggestions. Maximize your time and *invest* it wisely where your investment will produce the maximum return. You will then feel satisfied and accomplished. As you give of your time, you will then enhance your relationships (at home and at work). As a by-product, you will maximize your employees' talents.

Love the people, not the shoes.

PART III

MAXIMIZE YOUR TEAM'S TALENTS

NASCAR Racing and Strategic Planning: What it Takes to Win the Race

"A winning effort begins with preparation."

—JOE GIBBS

I f you are now reading Part III of this book, I hope you have enjoyed the journey of discovering and maximizing your talents as well as your employees' talents. I now want to take you in the journey where you and your employees can make things happen by maximizing the entire team's talents. To illustrate the concept, I share a story of remarkable team work and collaboration where everyone is in the right place and performing their individual jobs at their highest potential with one united purpose: to win the race.

The first time I attended a NASCAR (National Association for Stock Car Auto Racing) race, I went with my husband and son to Kansas City, Missouri. The experience was amazing and one I will never forget.

In the middle of the race, an amount of time passed when cars went lap after lap without any "cautions," meaning there were no wrecks. The drivers were doing so well that they drove one hundred laps with no incidents! I was bored to tears, I must admit. But then a lightbulb went on. I saw a clear analogy between NASCAR racing and strategic planning in regard to talent. Leaders must be strategic about the talent in their company and integrate talent management into their strategic plan. Everything from hiring the right talent from the start to retaining the right talent continually must be carefully and strategically planned. I share my observations as a result of the epiphany inspired by this experience.

Each race plan is important. It is important that each race team has a strategic plan that includes a vision of the team that *everyone* knows and understands. If the crew chief knows the plan but does not communicate it to the crew, they cannot support the driver. In the same way, you can't lead and run a company by yourself. You need your crew, and they need to know the specific strategies to win the race. Every person on the team has a job to do in order to win. If one lug nut on a wheel is not tight correctly, the car can lose that wheel and be out of the race. At a minimum, the driver will lose valuable time that can cost the victory. Each race is different and must have a specific plan to win each race. And each race counts toward the entire competition. In business, each year is different based on the economic factors affecting the world, the country, and each specific industry. Therefore, your company needs an updated strategic plan each year, and the entire team must know it well to succeed.

For your first race as the crew chief, Pastor Jared Van Voorst advises, "Listen and learn—especially in a new environment. People you are leading will not immediately trust you. Learn the culture first. Learn how the team works and builds their trust in you. There will also be times when you, as the leader, have to step in and help out. Doing so models humility to the team."

The driver is key but *not* the most important person on the team. The driver drives the car, but if the car is no good, neither the driver nor the team will go anywhere. The crew that prepares the car and supports the driver is integral to winning a race. For example, if their driver is in first place and goes to the pit for gas or to change tires and the crew is not fast and accurate, the driver can lose the first place easily in a matter of milliseconds—regardless of how many laps they were in first place.

Kevin Webb's advice for new leaders: "Show appreciation, be thankful, lead by example. Do the dirty work whether someone is watching or not—even if that includes picking up the garbage from the parking lot." One of his employees saw him doing just that and told him "You never cease to amaze me." Even though Kevin did it without thinking and was unaware of who was watching, this simple act had a powerful impact on his employee.

Constant communication is a must. Communicating the strategic plan to the entire organization is crucial for the company to win their "race." Knowing your employees' individual talents comes into play at this point. Each person must be placed at strategic places so they can work within their gifting and also know how important they are to the overall race or plan. Dr. Bekele Shanko said, "Knowing each person's talents helped us know how to manage those talents as a team."

At the NASCAR race, I noticed the constant communication on the ground among the team and between the "spotter" and the driver. The spotter is the team member up on the rooftop of the racetrack who alerts the driver of dangers and obstacles. Companies need spotters too. A leader needs to communicate with the leadership team, and they should communicate with the rest of the staff *continually* in order to keep the information flowing and the momentum going.

The NASCAR teams are very organized and orderly. They follow rules. Every game, every sport, every team, every industry has rules. The best players follow the rules. They take them seriously because there are consequences and penalties if they violate the rules. In NASCAR's case, someone can die if they don't follow the rules. Daily decisions in the marketplace may not be a matter of life or death, but the decisions leaders make do affect the lives of the employees.

In addition to rules, there is a specific order in which projects need to be managed. When several people become involved and don't work as a team, or when people (talent) are not placed in the right positions, chaos ensues, order turns to disorder, and goals are not met. The race is lost.

Team members watch each other's backs. Some things ahead can only be seen or felt by the driver. That person needs to communicate and alert the crew immediately of any trouble so they can come up with a plan of action. For example, the driver may be the only one to notice that something is wrong with the car. At the same time, only the spotter can see certain things and needs to alert the driver to watch out. For example, if the spotter sees a wreck on fire, he needs to inform the driver of whether it's okay to drive through the smoke. A driver who makes a bad move can wreck and completely lose the car and, in some instances, his or her life. The entire team loses—no car, no team. They must trust each other. The driver's life may depend on that trust.

The same happens in a company. Sometimes the leader and other times the staff sees something coming up that could affect the company's performance. It is important that you have identified who can replace or be a backup for other employees in case someone needs help or goes on vacation. When you know your team's talents, you can distribute the workload more effectively, each person utilizing their talents and skills for the best of the team—a perfect example of maximizing your team's talent and their individual talents.

Jen Ford Reedy suggests that to "Maximize an organization's talent, the leaders must build a culture of inclusivity—where every person feels they're contributing to the culture and also feel supported by the culture. To get the best out of people, they must know that they matter. They want to feel appreciated for what they bring."

Sometimes life is just not fair. You could say the race is not fair. One driver could have the lead for most of the race (even one hundred laps!) and lose at the very last minute because of a wreck caused by one bad move. The same happens in life. Your company can be doing well for many years and, all of a sudden, the unexpected happens. A key employee leaves, or the market crashes, or a new competitor comes to town. These moments are when you have an opportunity to start over or fix things that are broken or have been on hold for a while.

Continually innovate and do things differently. Have fun. For me, if there were no cautions and the cars just went around and around in circles, watching became boring. When there is no action or adventure, employees can fall into a routine and simply do the same thing repeatedly. They become unchallenged, customers become bored, leadership becomes stale, and you can lose your company's talent. That is time for a change and an opportunity to shift things around. Introduce new ideas and do things differently. When you rise out of the routine you may discover new talents you didn't know you had. Sometimes it's good to change things (maybe a process that needs improvement) in order to create and encourage innovation within the company. Innovation is fun. Without innovation in business, there is no action and life becomes boring. Gene Cross agrees, adding, "Your team must have fun. Otherwise, it's not a productive environment—even when you have a culture of accountability. Allow a team to enjoy each other. Welcome laughter in the team."

Finishing the race is what matters in the end. During this race, one driver went to the garage four times. Every time he started a lap, he had to go back to have something else fixed on his car. But in the end, he was persistent and finished the race. That mattered in the end. In fact, drivers are rewarded with points for every race they finish regardless of how many laps they were behind. What goes on their record is that they finished. The same happens in business. Every time a company tries something new and it doesn't work, the team needs to figure out new strategies to continue the race.

Never give up. Even though all the teams want to win the race and they all have strategies, there is only one winner. Only one driver and one team wins the trophy. Only one driver gets to do the "burnout" after taking the checkered flag! Sometimes, however, even when you have the best team and the best strategy for your business, life may throw a curve at you and your company, and you don't win. In those moments, remember past successes, gather your team, pick up the pieces (sometimes literally like in a car race) and, with your head up, start over. The most important thing is to never give up. Finish your race!

The team where each member
brings their shoes will win the race.

Leaders Connect
the Generations

"Coming together is a beginning. Keeping together is progress. Working together is success."

—Henry Ford

Regardless of how old you are or which generation you belong to, you will most likely work with various generations at the same time throughout your working life. As a leader, you work with employees, vendors, shareholders, customers, and all other stakeholders. You can be assured that you will encounter people of all ages and you need to learn to adjust your leadership style based mostly on people's personalities not so much based on their age.

Every generation brings different talents to the table, and we can maximize their individual talents at all levels and as a team. In my last job, I managed employees from ages twenty-three to sixty-seven—all in the same team. I treated them all fairly, yet differently. But not because of their ages. I treated them differently because each person is unique as an individual. I got to know them personally and molded my leadership and management style to each of them. I learned their personalities and identified their talents. Doing this really helped me understand their preferences for being recognized, rewarded, challenged, and staying committed.

In this chapter, I share how leaders can connect the generations by possessing certain characteristics to lead all generations successfully.

Work Ethic. What does it mean to have "work ethic"? It starts with respect for yourself and for others. It means you take your job seriously and conduct yourself with the utmost ethical behavior. It means you arrive to meetings on time to respect others' time. Being reliable and dependable as an employee and as a leader is a crucial component of your personal work ethic. Ensuring the tasks that you are entrusted with are done correctly and on time means you are a reliable person. If you tell a co-worker you will cover for him or her to finish a project, for example, and you come through as promised, that is being a dependable person which is part of your work ethic.

Work Hard. Working hard means you put your heart into everything you do, and you work with passion. Being efficient and effective at your job is a strategy that not many people apply in their lives. They think the leadership only sees you as hard-working person if you're physically in the office before and after regular working hours. But with technology, employees can work from home or away from the office and may get even more things done than if they were present in the office. As a leader, you need to work hard but not necessarily work long hours. Learn to be more efficient and effective at all you do and you will obtain higher results while avoiding burn out.

Be Patient. Leaders need to exercise patience daily. You need to learn to be patient with your employees in various ways. It takes time for new employees to learn their jobs and the culture of the organization. If you're leading employees who have been with the company for many years, then you'll need to be patient for them to learn the "new ways of doing things" as well as new technologies. Similarly, you need to be patient with yourself as you learn to lead for the first time. You will most likely make mistakes, but you can recover and move on. Lastly, it takes time to be promoted to higher levels of leadership so you will need to acquire more work experience and wait until the right opportunity comes along. Allow yourself to grow as a leader.

High Standards. What does it mean to have high

standards? It means you strive for excellence. Not good, not great, but excellent. Not perfection either because you are human and sometimes near perfect is all you'll be able to achieve. When you set high standards for yourself, you will be the example for your employees. The same way, when you expect high standards of your employees, they will follow your example.

Obtain Education. One of the best ways to maximize talents is by obtaining additional education. There are certain positions in a company that may require specialized education. As a leader, you need to provide your employees with the opportunities to learn and develop the skills necessary to do their jobs successfully. By doing so, you can then encourage them to strive for excellence. You can also develop yourself as a leader by attending leadership development training and reading leadership development books such as this one.

Significance. Regardless of people's ages and across generations, most people I know want to create significance in their workplace. Below are some suggestions on how you can connect the generations:

To younger generation leaders:

- Help, train, and teach the older generations technology and new ways of doing things.

- Respect the knowledge and expertise of the older workers and be open to learn from them.

- Be patient—both with the older workers as they learn the new technology and also patient as you wait to earn the privileges in the workplace that only come with years of work life experience.

To older generation leaders:

- Learn technology. Embrace it and use it to become more efficient and effective in your work.

- Respect young workers as they also know a lot and have valuable perspectives.

- Teach young workers what you know about work life experience.

- Be open to learn from the younger workers.

To leaders of any generation:

- Become the connector of generations. Be a bridge!

- Learn from all generations.

- Mentor younger workers and be mentored by older workers.

We are all different and unique, yet we all want these main things.

- To feel valued
- To be significant

- To be recognized for our work
- To contribute to society

When you discover the talents of your employees plus add the unique life experiences each generation brings, you recognize that you have an amazing team and vast knowledge to draw from. Take advantage of the people from all generations who can and are willing to work at your company. Together they create a deep pool of talent that can make your company more successful than ever.

I want to encourage working people from all generations to work together as one team. Age should not matter. What matters is that we work together to accomplish the vision of the companies we work for.

There are shoes for every season . . .
We need them all in our closet.

Leaders and Athletes: What They Have in Common

"Leaders influence others through words, but most importantly, by their example."

—Marcia Malzahn

What does it take to be a leader? What does it take to be an athlete? When we think of athletes, we think of teams because typically athletes are part of a team. But we also know that each athlete must perform individually for the entire team to win. Additionally, we associate athletes with being leaders in their respective sports. If you were to refer to your employees as *athletes*, what kind of athletes are you training for your team? Are they playing the sport that matches their physical abilities? Are you maximizing their athletic abilities by placing them in the right positions? And, are some of those athletes also leaders in their field? In this chapter, I describe similarities between leaders and athletes so you can identify areas you may need to develop as a leader.

Many traits of successful leaders spill over into other areas of their lives, such as fitness. Similarly, many of the traits that successful athletes display can also make a person a successful leader. So, when comparing leaders and athletes (or simply people who are physically fit), I came up with fifteen traits they have in common.

Dedication. It takes an incredible amount of dedication to continually grow as a leader and hone your skills. Equally, it takes an amazing amount of dedication to be fit—and stay fit—throughout your life. Sometimes athletes have setbacks, like an injury that needs to heal for several weeks. Leaders have setbacks as well, such as losing their jobs, but they get up and keep trying. What matters is that they are each dedicated to succeeding. They are persistent.

Goals. Leaders set goals and work hard to attain those goals. Athletes set goals as well. Each day, each week, month, and year, they strive to improve at their sport. They track their progress and celebrate the small successes as they reach their goals. Leaders do the same. They set goals for themselves as well as for the organizations or groups they lead. Leaders and athletes are each focused on their goals. When athletes belong to a team, they participate in setting their team goals in addition to their personal goals. Just as in sports, business leaders participate in setting the company goals, and they also have their personal goals. When I asked Kevin Webb how he's maximized his team's talents, he said, "By providing opportunities and promoting their independence, and by having lots of goals."

Discipline. Discipline is different than dedication. Discipline is doing things consistently and usually at the same time each day so you establish a routine. You can be disciplined to do a specific task consistently, but you may not be dedicated to it if your heart is not in it. It takes discipline to schedule your workout, attend a seminar, or read a book in order to improve your skills—both as an athlete and as a leader. Dedication and discipline work together to make good things happen.

Sacrifice. Leaders, just like athletes, make daily sacrifices in order to excel and be successful. Of course, it's probably more fun to go out with friends for a drink or go shopping, but leaders and athletes see the long-term goal. They have a vision of the finish line and know this is a journey with successes and failures along the way. It takes daily sacrifice and a lifestyle commitment to get to every finish line.

Patience. Leaders and athletes are patient. Before you can experience results in any area of your life, you must put in the work, the time, the dedication, discipline, and sacrifice. As mentioned in the previous chapter, you need to be patient with yourself and with your staff. Let your employees grow and develop within their abilities. Similarly, athletes must be patient with improving their athletic ability and also to wait for the other team members to improve—both individually and as a team.

When I asked Greg Shamey in what areas new leaders could use the most help, he said, "I think patience is important. It's very tempting coming in as a new leader and creating your stamp on the organization to show your value right away. Getting to know the people and the customers and sharing that you're new and you don't know everything are key to success as a new leader. Don't try to overhaul everything at once. Make changes as you build trust with your employees and customers. Take the information and make informed decisions."

Heidi Gesell advises new managers and leaders to "take time to learn about your team. Really listen to what they're telling you and don't make any changes for at least six months. Be sincere with your team."

Results. Both leaders and athletes want results. They strive to achieve the results they set out for. The results when you are fit are not only a healthy body but a positive attitude and increased self-esteem and self-confidence. When you are an effective leader, results are the satisfaction you get when you see those you lead grow and become successful. You also feel satisfaction when you see a vision realized. When you maximize your team's talents in your company you will see results.

Jeanne Crain advises leaders to "connect everyone through commitment and alignment, making sure the team is aware of where you want to go and what you want to achieve. It's about communicating the 'why' and understanding that the whole is better than just one person."

Drive. Leaders and athletes have the drive to go on. It's an inner fire that is hard to quench. Some people don't have it and don't understand what drives leaders and athletes. When you ask leaders why they do what they do, they may respond simply, "Because I want to be the best leader I can be." An athlete may answer, "Because I want my team to win, or because I want to win the gold medal."

Inspiration. Leaders inspire others to be the best they can be. In the same way, athletes inspire the young and old to "go for it." Every time I watch the Olympics, I get inspired to improve and encouraged to continue the hard work to remain physically fit. Leaders and athletes inspire others just by being themselves, by their own example of how they live their lives.

Influence. Leaders are influential because they inspire you to do something. They engage you on the idea of their vision. They help you change your life. They encourage you to grow and help you grow. Athletes also inspire others to get in shape. But when it comes to working out, only you can do it for your body. As a leader, when it comes to personal development, only you can do it for yourself. You must desire to grow and take the initiative to improve.

Encouragement. Leaders and athletes, many times without knowing, encourage others to improve their lives. At the same time, they also need encouragement from others to continue their journey. Sometimes we forget that leaders and athletes have feelings too, and it takes courage to lead, the same way it takes courage to continually train to stay fit for competition.

Balance. Leaders and athletes strive to be balanced individuals. They understand that balance is achievable, but it takes a lot of discipline, short-term and long-term sacrifices, and daily choices. They don't compare themselves to others because they are also clear as to what balance means to *them*. They take into consideration everything in their life including their capacity to handle various situations and workloads—both at home and at work. They know their limitations, establish boundaries, and have their priorities straight. Lastly, they strive to balance their entire being—physical, emotional, and spiritual.

Listen. Leaders and athletes learn to listen. Leaders learn the business and get to know their employees by listening to them, as a group and individually. They ask open ended questions and then pause to listen to responses. Athletes learn the rules of the game and get to know their team mates by listening and paying attention to the strategies to win the game. Greg Shamey shared, "Getting to know the team is the first thing I did as a new leader. What motivates you and your career? Do you enjoy your current job? Are you looking for that next promotion? Are you looking to get a certification? Are you looking to be known more in the organization? Do you want to be a leader someday? It's all about listening and being a resource and advocate for your employees. It's important to set that tone right from the start."

Dr. Bekele Shanko shared a similar view. "The advice I always give to new leaders is this: before you lead, you must listen. Understand the history of the organization before you propose any vision, listen to all stakeholders, understand their dreams, frustrations, and their expectations of your leadership. Don't lead alone. Lead with the people in the organization. Don't just bring your vision but go through a process of listening and develop a shared vision. Then you will be successful."

Coach. Everyone needs a coach and successful leaders and athletes have professional coaches. A coach is different than a mentor in that you pay for coaching. Mentoring, on the other hand, is free. A coach will encourage you and keep you accountable for the goals you set out to do. You are in charge of setting your own goals, and a coach will help you by coaching you to achieve them. A mentor is someone who comes alongside you to share his or her similar experiences to help you in your journey. They may or may not be in your same industry and they may mentor you in various areas of your life. Dr. Bekele Shanko believes that "new leaders need to be helped to develop a habit of self-reflection, take personal assessment tests, and be coached by experienced leaders."

Resilient. When you look at the lives of long-term successful leaders and athletes, you will notice that those who continue their journey regardless of all the obstacles and adversities they encounter, are resilient. Resilience is the ability to overcome adversity in your life. If you ever wondered why some people make it and some don't, that is the answer. Some people possess the ability to bounce back, and overcome failures, depression, and adversity in their lives. I'm paraphrasing the definition of resilience from the Dictionary.com.

Example. Everyone needs a positive example to improve their lives. Leaders and athletes are examples of all the attributes described above. They both feel a huge responsibility to be a *positive* example to others watching them. Otherwise, their negative example can have devastating consequences for their followers. This holds true for people who lead corporations or causes of any size as well as athletes who are looked up to by millions of people—usually by youth. Therefore, being an example is probably the most important responsibility for leaders and athletes. If you are a leader and/or an athlete, take the responsibility seriously.

As a business leader, you have a tremendous responsibility to be an example to other leaders (in addition to your employees) and display all the traits described above. As a leader, you have the responsibility to first discover and develop your talents, then to discover and help your employees develop their talents. And lastly, you have the opportunity to maximize all of those talents together for the benefit of the entire company. Leaders influence others through words, but most importantly, by their example.

What areas do you feel you need to develop? I encourage you to look for a coach to guide you through the process.

Even when your team wears the same kind of shoes . . .
yours are still your individual size.

Traits of a Leader,
Traits of a Follower

*"The quality, not the longevity, of one's life is
what is important."*

—MARTIN LUTHER KING

Some people think leaders have it easy, that they do their own thing and are accountable to no one. Others may think leaders started out being leaders—born that way. But that is not the case. Being a leader is an enormous responsibility, and it's not easy. Most leaders start as followers and worked hard to be where they are today—even if they had the natural ability of leadership in them from the start. In fact, successful leaders are also excellent followers. Being a good follower is precisely what gives great leaders the foundation to be an example of integrity, humility, honesty, and many of the other traits that we admire in successful leaders. Next are some key traits of successful followers.

They need a teacher, a leader. Followers need to follow someone they trust and believe in—someone worthy of being followed.

Followers don't doubt their leader. They have complete faith that their leader has his or her best interest at heart. They don't fear that their leader is out to get them.

Good followers get to know their leader on a personal level. They understand their leader is also human and has a need for personal relationships too.

Good followers learn to appreciate their leaders for who they are. They are not "apple polishers." They sincerely care for their leader.

Followers gather together to support their common leader. They don't talk behind his or her back, and they are loyal to their leader.

Good followers "do" what their leader tells them to do. They don't second-guess or question their leader each time he or she asks them to do something. In the business arena, of course, it is acceptable to ask questions to clarify direction and to bring your opinion but, in the end, good followers learn to do what is asked of them (unless it's something illegal or unethical).

A good leader influences followers and **the followers**

allow themselves to be influenced. It's a mutual relationship based on trust, something that is becoming less common in the workplace.

Leaders give authority to their followers without fear that they will misuse that authority. Again, this exercise of giving authority to others is based on trust. **Good followers accept that authority and use it wisely.**

Followers admire and look up to their leader. They want to and aspire to be like their leader. They are proud of their leader and not ashamed. They want to imitate their leader and become more like him or her.

Successful followers receive instructions from their leader and work together to accomplish their common mission (or the vision of their company). They learn to use their various strengths and talents as a team to get things done.

Now, let's examine some of the traits we admire— and even expect—of successful leaders:

Leaders have the innate ability to influence others—at the core, that's what leadership is about. Even though not everyone is born with the leadership gift or ability, every person who is in a leadership position can learn to be an amazing and influential leader. You *can* and should develop your leadership ability.

Leaders are learners. Most successful leaders are life-long learners. They have a hunger for knowledge and enjoy the journey of learning. They also love to teach what they have learned. They don't mind sharing their knowledge with others as they don't feel threatened because they have a high self-esteem and self-confidence. They develop their own talents to become strengths. Because they also like to teach others, they naturally develop those they lead.

Leaders have a good attitude toward life, which is manifested in their attitude and behavior at work and at home. They know they cannot control circumstances but *can* control their own attitude. They know they are the full beneficiaries of the change in their attitude.

Leaders are hard workers and work efficiently and effectively. Regardless of the career they choose, leaders work hard. This doesn't mean they work 90–100 hours a week, which some people do. What this means is that they invest their time wisely and have learned to manage their time successfully based on their values. They have learned to delegate and thus develop the talents of those they lead. They work efficiently by using technology appropriately and they work effectively by investing their time in the right activities.

They focus their time on what's most important— *consistently*. The key here is that they learned to say "no" to the things that clutter their lives with no significant impact or influence. And they say "yes" to the things that matter.

Most leaders are also followers. If you are a new leader, choose to also be a good follower. Only then will you become a true influential person. Only then will you leave a legacy of goodwill in the lives of all the people you touch along the way. Therefore, choose carefully who you follow, and choose to be the best leader you were meant to be.

Good quality shoes are worth every penny.

Leaders Leading Leaders

"If we are together nothing is impossible. If we are divided all will fail."

—WINSTON CHURCHILL

Let's recap what we have discussed in this book. Starting with the end in mind to "bring *YOUR* shoes," meaning bring *your* talents and your entire self to every job. We began with the first steps—discovering and maximizing *your* talents. Then we moved on to discovering and maximizing the talents of those you lead. Lastly, we want to maximize the talent of your team—as a whole.

I want you to think about repeating this cycle over and over in order to perpetuate your company's legacy. You need to focus on training your leaders, so they can in turn train their leaders and so on—*leaders leading leaders*.

Let's describe the steps you need to go through in order to maximize your team's talents.

Identify your future leaders. I've seen a growing trend where new leaders are promoted to senior leadership and even executive leadership positions even though they've never supervised before! If this is your case, don't panic. The advice in this book is designed precisely to help new leaders, and that includes you. But regardless of your experience, the first step is to identify the future leaders of the company or the department you lead.

If you are a new leader and your job is a senior or executive leadership position, or if you're managing a division or a department of the company, you need to identify the successors. Sometimes the people that you have in the current positions are not necessarily the future leaders of those specific divisions or teams. In this process, you need to consider the team's capabilities, leadership ability, and maturity/capability of the members to take on new leadership responsibilities. Some key traits that the leaders I interviewed look for consistently in future leaders are strong communication skills, the willingness and ability to collaborate, integrity, humility, compassion, enthusiasm, and honesty.

Develop your leaders. Once you identify the future leaders, spend time with them and help them develop themselves as leaders and/or provide them with opportunities to grow. Every leader needs to develop their individual talents, their leadership ability, management skills, and delegation skills in order to succeed and move forward with an organization. An outside coach may be necessary to help develop a particular leader. Kevin Webb would like to see "more outside coaching to tell employees the same thing you may be telling them but in a different way, from an outside perspective."

Jeanne Crain advises leaders who are leading leaders to "Create opportunities for new managers to learn from each other. There is safety in that. Understand others may have the same insecurities. As a company, you must leverage talent for the benefit of your customers."

Learn to delegate. Delegation is not a talent. It's a critical skill you must learn to succeed as a leader. There are several reasons to delegate.

1. **Delegate to save time.** For every task you have to do as a leader, ask yourself the question, "Can someone else perform this task?" If the answer is yes, delegate that task. It may at first require you to train the person you're delegating to, but you will save time almost immediately.

2. **Delegate to develop your team.** As part of developing your employees, you must delegate tasks and functions that you may feel are a stretch for them. But they will appreciate the opportunity and will welcome the additional responsibility. You must

ensure, however, that the employee doesn't feel you're dumping on them. You need to delegate effectively and appropriately. This means you train the person, give them the tools needed to perform the task successfully, and also ensure that the employee has the time available to do the new task. You may also have to move current tasks from this employee to another one to provide adequate time for the new tasks/function.

3. **Delegate to earn your employees' trust.** I've always told my employees that in order for them to grow as a leader, they will need to delegate many functions they love to do. Otherwise, they will not grow themselves. It takes trust to delegate tasks—especially crucial functions that must be done correctly and have little room for error. Therefore, you must choose the right employee to delegate these sensitive or complex tasks. Providing the right training and appropriate time to perform these new functions will ensure a successful transition.

4. **Delegate to create a backup for yourself.** One of the worst feelings when one goes on vacation is knowing that no one can do your job or certain parts of your job while you're gone. While this may create a false sense of job security, the stress of knowing that a pile of work is waiting for you when you

return takes away from the fun of being on vacation. By delegating those critical tasks, you will be able to go away in peace knowing your department is running smoothly while you take time away to refresh.

5. **Delegate to create new efficiencies.** As a leader, it is imperative that you spend your time on the most important activities. Those include strategic planning, hiring the right people, developing your employees, and nurturing your relationships within your company and customers or other stakeholders. Delegating will give you the time to focus on the most critical aspects of your leadership job.

Greg Shamey shared his "best" advice for new leaders as they start their leadership journey, saying, "You don't have to do everything yourself. You have this whole team to leverage and their talents to use. Influence and inspire your team to obtain the results you desire together. Get to know the other leaders of the organization. Create a culture of collaboration with other areas of the organization. Be authentic and genuine. It's okay to say you don't know everything."

Demonstrate leadership. Allow your leaders to follow their own passions, which are tied to their talents and personal mission or purpose. As stressed previously, ensure that the leaders you're leading share the company's values. Otherwise, they're not the right people to begin with. Teach them to develop their own leaders within the departments they lead. Everyone should understand the organization's mission—the reason "why" you exist. Everyone should also understand the significance of their job and ideally everyone feels the same "passion for the purpose." Again, communicate the vision continually and in various ways so everyone knows where you're going, what you want to become, and where you want to go together as a company. As a team, you can now focus on following your mission and accomplish your overall company's vision.

Erin Procko believes leaders must demonstrate that "they care deeply about their employees and customers and always put them first." Secondly, she believes leaders should be able to "inspire people to fulfill the organization's vision . . . It isn't easy or comfortable every day, but if employees feel good about what they are doing and where we are going, then they can be empowered and work hard together."

The Power of TEAM. As you demonstrate leadership to your team, you can show them the power they have as a team to overcome challenges together. You can celebrate overcoming those challenges. You will achieve success and take risks together—and celebrate through the journey achieving the individual successes. Remind them that *ordinary* people can form an *extraordinary* team. First, bring *your* shoes to the job. Bring your unique abilities and maximize them. Why? So you can help others. Then, remind your team members to bring *their* shoes as well so they can also help others. Help them discover their talents and give them opportunities to maximize those talents. Why? Because you may have a superstar in your midst and you may miss it if you don't know their talents and allow them to develop those talents.

Lastly, maximize your team's talents. Why? Because we're all here to fulfill our purpose. Together, discovering, using, and maximizing our talents, we can do it. You can now say you are a *leader leading leaders* by maximizing talent. You are now all bringing *your* shoes!

An extraordinary team can wear ordinary shoes
and still get the job done!

Epilogue

My desire is for this book to serve as a practical guide to help new leaders succeed. I hope the ideas offered in this book inspire you to use your unique talents and combination of experiences and skills to be the best leader *you* can be—and to be okay being *you* as you take on your new leadership role. I also hope you feel encouraged to discover and maximize your talents and the talents of those you lead, and lastly, maximize the *talent* of your entire team. Knowing yourself well and knowing those you lead is how you can work together to maximize an organization's talent. You, as a leader, can achieve a higher level of success, satisfaction, and fulfillment in your organization.

When you maximize your talents to help others and allow those you lead to do the same, you may not only discover a superstar but you will influence more people through your employees. In the end, we're all here to fulfill our unique purpose, and together we can help each other to accomplish that.

I wish you and your organization much success. My hope is that you are encouraged to be who you are as a unique individual with your talents, so you can always *Bring YOUR Shoes*!

Your next step? If you don't feel comfortable in *your* shoes, I'm here to help! You can contact me to explore coaching opportunities through my website www.malzahn strategic.com or email me at marcia@marciamalzahn.com.

Acknowledgments

I thank my husband, Tim Malzahn, for allowing me to discover my talents and giving me the opportunity to maximize those talents—especially now that I'm working on my consulting practice, speaking, and writing. When I left my twenty-three-year banking career, it was to pursue my life's purpose, my calling. Writing this book to help leaders is part of fulfilling my calling, using one of my bigger talents—writing.

I want to acknowledge my long-time boss and friend, Reid Evenson, who saw my potential and talents since I was twenty-one years old. He hired me to work for him in cash management at a bank. We worked together for thirteen years; and five years after I had left banking, he hired me again to start a community bank. He gave me the amazing opportunity to use and he helped me maximize every talent I had. Thank you, Reid! I will forever be grateful to you.

I thank my other boss, Jeanne Crain, who also saw talents in me and decided to take a chance on me. Thank you, Jeanne, for giving me the very first job as a branch manager even though I had never supervised anyone. You saw in me the leadership gift and gave me that wonderful opportunity to lead in the workplace. Lastly, I thank Pastor Mac Hammond who again saw leadership talent in me in addition to other gifts that helped the church when I worked there. He gave me the opportunity to lead the IT, HR, and Finance departments of the church he founded. Again I had no experience leading a nonprofit, and he gave me the chance because he believed in me. Thank you!

Thank you to the following friends and leaders who read the unedited version of this book to give me their honest feedback and make it the best it could be for *you*: Ruth Johnson, CEO of Homes for Heroes; Keith Adams, retired leader; Laura Adams, one of my previous employees and friend; Nichol Beckstrand, president and CEO of Minnesota Multi-Housing Association; Blake Kloeckner, director of Finance at ThreeBridge, and also one of my trusted employees; Reid Evenson, CEO of Tradition Bancshares, Inc. and my ex-boss; Doug Hile, retired bank executive and Board member, James Hushagen, attorney with Eisenhour Carlson, PLLP, Karen Himle, senior vice president Customer Experience and Corporate Affairs at Thrivent Financial, and my husband, Tim Malzahn, who read it several times.

Thank you to the following leaders who gave me their time to interview them to include their wisdom in this book: Heidi Gesell, president and CEO of Bank Cherokee, Jen Ford Reedy, president of Bush Foundation, Jeanne Crain, president and CEO of Bremer Financial Corporation, Nichol Beckstrand, president and CEO of Minnesota Multi-Housing Association, Melissa Johnston, senior vice president of Commercial Banking at Highland Bank, Aleesha Webb, president and vice chairwoman of the board of Village Bank, Gene Cross, Commercial Banking leader and consultant, Dr. Bekele Shanko, vice president, Global Church Movements, CRU, Kevin Webb, founder and president, All American Title Company, Pastor Jared Van Voorst, Hosanna Church, Greg Shamey, director of Charitable Planning, inFaith Community Foundation, and Erin Procko, Minneapolis president and Twin Cities Banking director of Bell Bank.

Special thanks for author David McNally for writing the Foreword. David is author of *Even Eagles Need a Push*, a leadership book that helped me when I was starting my leadership journey. His book helped me realize that I was an eagle and that I needed a push. Years later, David wrote a best-selling sequel, *Mark of an Eagle: How Your Life Changes the World*, which also impacted my leadership journey. Another special thanks to Julie Peterson Klein, executive vice president and chief culture officer of Bell Bank, and Chris Kelly, president and founder of AssetHR, for reading the pre-final version of the book and providing me with their testimonial about the book.

Thank you all for helping me put this book together with the purpose to equip new leaders. You are an example of how leaders lead leaders—by maximizing your team's talents and *bringing YOUR shoes* wherever you go.

About the Author

Marcia (Marci) Malzahn is a wife, mother, writer, author, and professional speaker as well as a successful entrepreneur, and small business owner. She started four businesses, climbed the corporate ladder, and has experience both in the for-profit and the nonprofit world. Marci is president of Malzahn Strategic, a community financial institution consulting practice focusing on strategic planning, enterprise risk management, treasury management, and talent management.

Considered a business leader in the Minneapolis/St. Paul community, Marcia was the recipient of several awards including "25 On the Rise," given by the Minnesota Hispanic Chamber of Commerce to successful Minnesota Hispanics under age forty. *Minneapolis/St. Paul Business Journal* named her one of the "40 Under Forty." *Finance and Commerce* newspaper named her one of the "Top Women in Finance," and *Northwestern Financial Review Magazine* (now *BankBeat* Magazine) gave her the "Outstanding Women in Banking" Award. Marci was also featured in the *Minnesota Business Magazine* as one of the "Minnesota Immigrant Success Stories."

Marci is the author of *Devotions for Working Women: A Daily Inspiration to Live a Successful and Balanced Life* (Expert Publishing, Inc., 2006), *The Fire Within: Connect Your Gifts with Your Calling* (Malzahn Publishing, 2015), and *The Friendship Book: Because You Matter to Me* (Malzahn Publishing, 2016) also in Spanish, *El Libro de la Amistad: Porque Tu Me Importas* (Malzahn Publishing, 2017). Marci was featured in the book, *Green Card Entrepreneur Voices* (2018), which she co-authored.

Marcia is also founder of Crowning Achievements International, her speaking business, with the mission of pursuing excellence in the financial services community. As a professional international bilingual (English/Spanish) speaker, Marci speaks frequently at banking conferences and associations, women's leadership conferences, and faith-based events. She is also an online/webinar trainer on banking and leadership topics. Marci is a certified life coach from the Lifeforming Institute. Marci holds a BA in Business Management from Bethel University and is a graduate and faculty member of the Graduate School of Banking, Madison, Wisconsin, and the South West Graduate School of Banking in Dallas, Texas.

Marcia's personal mission is to help working people to be successful in every area of their lives. She and her husband Tim live in Minnesota and have two grown children.

Marcia's Other Works

Marci started writing in 2004, and she is not planning on stopping any time soon. Because Marci has always been a full-time working woman, she wanted to inspire other working women to be successful while striving to achieve balance in their lives. That led her to publish her first book in 2006, *Devotions for Working Women: A Daily Inspiration to Live a Successful and Balanced Life*.

Several years later in 2015, Marci founded Malzahn Publishing, and published her second book, *The Fire Within: Connect Your Gifts with Your Calling*. Through this book, Marci inspires and encourages her readers to discover their gifts, polish them, and use them to help others. Marci takes you

in a journey to connect your gifts with your purpose and calling in life.

In April 2016, Marci published her third book, *The Friendship Book: Because You Matter to Me*, and dedicated it to all her friends around the world. Marci treasures  her friendships, and in this book she inspires others to appreciate and nurture their friendships. This book is meant to be given as a gift to your friends.

Marci published this special little friendship book in Spanish, *El Libro de la Amistad,* an especially wonderful gift for adults and teens who are learning Spanish!

You can find Marci's books on her website www.marcia malzahn.com or www.amazon.com.